Forgotten
A Memoir

Living in the Shadows of
Domestic Violence

TIFFANY MENSAH

Mensah Co. Publishing
Phoenix, AZ

FORGOTTEN: LIVING IN THE SHADOWS
OF DOMESTIC VIOLENCE

This book is based on true events. The author has tried to recreate events, locales, and conversations from memory. To maintain anonymity, the author has changed the names of individuals and places. Some events have been slightly altered for confidentiality, and some dialogue has been recreated.

This publication is designed to educate and provide general information regarding the subject matter based on the author's experiences. It is published with the understanding that neither the author nor the publisher is engaged in rendering professional counseling services. Each situation is different, and the advice should be tailored to particular circumstances.

ISBN-13: 978-0-578-62199-9

Published by Mensah Co. Publishing
Phoenix, AZ

Printed in the United States of America
First Edition February 2020

Design: Sirocki and Make Your Mark Publishing Solutions
Editing: Make Your Mark Publishing Solutions

Acknowledgements

GRATITUDE AND THANKFULNESS FLOOD my heart to the God who created me and gave me the gifting, courage, and strength to write this book from a place of healing and wholeness.

My husband, AJ, being married to you is the greatest gift since salvation. It is also proof that God loves me so much that He created you for me and has shown me what healthy love can be and look like. There aren't enough words to say thank you for pushing me to continue with this project. Thank you for rolling up your sleeves and digging into this book with me to ensure it's the best it can be. You're my biggest cheerleader, and I love you with my whole heart. #teamthree baby!

Dedication

To the survivors of domestic violence and the memory of
those who have lost their lives due to domestic violence.

To the children who had to endure their parents' domestic
violence or have lost a parent to domestic violence.

To those who are on the frontlines, fighting against domestic violence.

You all are not Forgotten.

Introduction

I STARED OUT THE window of my bedroom while the crisp breeze brushed my face. I leaned on the ledge, gazing at the neighborhood kids as they raced down the street on their bikes with smiles painted across their faces. My mind drifted into wonder. *What would it be like if he changed this time? What if he never hit my mom anymore? What if he realizes he's wrong and won't do this to our family anymore? Or what if he never comes back home? What if he realizes he can't change, and he just leaves so none of us will hurt anymore?*

I often fantasized about us being happy like we once were, imagining a new version of our family, creating new memories without my dad in the picture. Fantasies of no longer being a prisoner in my home, being able to join the neighborhood kids racing down the street with no cares.

It only took for his navy blue Lincoln to turn onto our street and creep past the corner house into the view of my bedroom window to snap me back into reality and for disappointment to flood my soul. I lowered my blinds, hoping he didn't catch me in the window. I sat on the edge of my bed to ponder on what version of my dad was coming home for the day.

Happy Dad or Angry Dad?

I waited for him to pull into the driveway, for the small pause before the garage opened for him to drive in and park, to get out of the car and open the door to the backseat and grab his

ix

lunch box. I held my breath as he closed the car door, shut the garage then walked to the gate to close it. Finally, after a short eternity, he came into the house.

I was ready and waiting for the sounds that would determine if it was safe to come out of my room. I had learned to use my ears like a sonar to paint a picture of the environment outside my bedroom door. Was I in friendly territory today, or would I be in a war zone? I never knew what to expect.

If I heard my dad's laughter from the kitchen within the first two minutes, it was safe to come out. But if the first two minutes lapsed into silence or elevated voices, my dad yelling and slamming things, it was an indicator to stay put in my room barricaded behind the door.

I waited to see what happened. If he went directly into my parents' bedroom, I'd quietly sneak out from behind enemy lines to scurry downstairs, keeping my distance until I heard his snores rumbling through the floor under their bedroom.

I was caught in a vicious cycle, our daily routine—wash, rinse, and repeat. My dad was the terrorist in our home day and night, and our family was a prisoner of war.

We didn't live in a home of peace, especially when on the run from my dad. As the youngest, I was forced to go with my mom as she fled for safety from the beatings my dad handed out at the most unsuspecting times. During these mad dashes for asylum, I was introduced to the feelings of abandonment, being forgotten, disregarded, and flat out unloved by my mother. I was often mislabeled and treated badly by those to whom we fled for safety. Those experiences made me angry, unforgiving, and hateful. I sought escape through pointless sex, toxic relationships, and controlling others, all outward cries to get someone to take the time to see me as a victim, too, like they saw my mom. We were both victims, but, somehow, I was always treated like unwanted baggage. I became a fighter with a warrior complex, fighting for myself physically and verbally. I was determined to prove to those who had mislabeled me that they were wrong about me.

What else is there to do when a situation you have no control over seemingly erases you from the minds of your caregivers? When you're forgotten by the ones who brought you into the world. Dismissed by the people who are supposed to love and care for you. Put on the back burner by the ones charged with providing you an atmosphere of peace and safe shelter. I was desperate for my voice to be heard by those who wouldn't, couldn't, or didn't care enough to hear.

Over fifteen million children are exposed to domestic violence yearly, and forty million adults grew up in these households. I am one of the statistics—I, too, was a victim. I wasn't physically abused, but I was hit with the repercussions and collateral damage. I was right there with my mom, subjected to all the violence, pulled out of my home time and time again only to endure the verbal tirades of family and so-called friends who were supposedly providing safe havens for us.

I was one of the *Forgotten*.

Everyone has a story to tell. I want to give a voice to those we sometimes don't get to hear. Those who feel forgotten, not purposely, but overlooked. Those who have been mislabeled or don't know how to internally process what they've seen or gone through. It is my heart's desire to start a conversation and bring these voices to the table, the ones closest to the victim—the children.

I choose to tell my story because it holds the key to someone else's victory. I will share the healing journey I embarked upon to realign my life and become emotionally healthy by addressing the trauma I endured and witnessed.

It took a while for me to get there because, for many years, I felt God was punishing me, and I wondered why my life had to be so difficult. I came to realize my pain had purpose. The hard times I faced early in my life had nothing to do with me. They were the consequences of choices others had made; however, as an adult, I had a choice: continue to blame and not heal or heal and take accountability for my self-sabotaging actions. While going through the fire of life, I endured burns and, at times, couldn't see my way through, but I didn't succumb to it. I made it through alive and better.

I love my mother and dad equally despite our difficult life. This book was not written to expose them or put them in a negative light; however, it is important that I share my story to encourage others. With this book, I will deliver truth and transparency.

This is my story, a child who grew up with domestic violence—the *Forgotten*.

The First Time

It seemed like a normal Saturday afternoon, my mom folding clothes in my parents' bedroom while my sister, Mallory, and I sat in the living room doing homework. It was around one p.m. Mallory and I were sharing a good laugh at one of her many silly jokes between homework problems when the back door swung open and quickly slammed shut. The blinds rattled frantically against the door. My sister and I were perplexed as our dad rushed through the kitchen and past the living room, hooking an abrupt left. He turned the corner, rushing toward my parents' bedroom. My heart was beating through my chest. We hadn't even heard our dad pull up, and we couldn't grasp why he'd come into the house so aggressively and in a rush.

He slammed the bedroom door behind him and began yelling at my mom. We knew our parents argued; we'd heard that before, but we weren't prepared for what we heard shortly after. We tried to go back to doing our homework, but we heard furniture being tossed, my mom's screams, and my dad's booming voice growing louder.

Mallory and I froze at the sound of shattering glass.

What is happening? I thought, looking at Mallory in silence with fearful eyes. She stared back at me with matched fear.

Our mother ran out of the bedroom, trying to make her way into the bathroom so she could lock herself inside, but my dad was close behind her. He grabbed her arm and tackled her in the middle of the hallway. Mallory and I sat still, watching with terror in our hearts and fear in our eyes as our dad turned our mom over onto her back. She tried to put up a fight, but he grabbed her arms with his gigantic hand while slapping her with the other as she screamed.

He continued to hit her while telling her to shut up. As he lay on top of her, I could hear my mom gasping for breath between escalating screams and pleas for him to stop. He shifted to put his hand over her mouth to silence her.

With tears falling from my face, I yelled, "Daddy, stop!"

Mallory quickly came out of her frozen state and rushed into action, swiftly jumping up from the table to pull me into her room.

"Tiff, no, be quiet. You don't know what he could do to us next."

I felt afraid for my mom and helpless. *What if he kills her? He's hurting her so bad.*

I wanted to do something, but I didn't know how, so we sat in my sister's room, crying. I held my legs up to my face as I cried tears filled with angst and anxiety. Guilt and helplessness weighed me down, but suddenly, I found some courage and I decided to do something. Mallory's room was a staircase jump to the kitchen. I hopped to the kitchen as quickly as I could and grabbed the phone from the wall to call Tyler, my second oldest brother who was away at college.

The wait for him to pick up the phone seemed like forever. My heart was banging in my chest. My nerves had me trembling. It seemed like time had stopped. I hoped my dad didn't come into the kitchen to catch me in the act.

Finally, Tyler answered.

"Tyler," I whispered while crying. "Daddy came home and

jumped on Mama. Me and Mallory had to hide in Mallory's room."

He seemed speechless for a beat. "Is that them?" he asked, referring to the violent noises that surrounded me.

"Yes." He went silent again. "Hello? You there?" I whispered.

"Yeah, I'm here," he replied with a broken voice on the verge of tears.

"Tiff, go back into Mallory's room and stay there. I gotta go."

I gently hung the phone up on the wall so I wouldn't alert my dad and tiptoed back into Mallory's room, scooting into a corner.

Her room didn't offer any solace. There were two doors, the door closest to the back door, which also led to the basement and kitchen, and the other door, which faced the hallway across from the bathroom. We were right next to the chaos going on in the middle of the hallway, in clear ear shot of our parents' turmoil.

We could now hear what had triggered my dad's erratic behavior. My mom had called my dad's friend, a man he worked with who was another minister, and asked him for prayer, which was a huge no-no. My dad didn't allow my mom to even acknowledge other men, let alone call them. He took it as proof that she was sleeping with his friend or wanted him to be her boyfriend.

"You're crazy! That's not true! Get off me. You're hurting me. Get off me!" my mom yelled.

"Nah, you want him to be your man. You want his prayers. You're sleeping with him!" my dad repeated between ragged breaths.

"That's not true. Get off me!"

We stayed in the room while our dad beat our mom for what seemed like hours. The punches paused momentarily as my mom continued to plead for our dad to release her.

"I ain't going nowhere," he said as he continued to curse her out.

When he finally got up, he went into their bedroom and slammed the door. We could hear our mom lying there crying before finally making her way to the bathroom to lock herself in.

We gave it some time before coming out of the room, but when we did, it looked like a tornado had swept through the back half of the house. The hallway was a mess, where he'd initially started, leading down to the entryway of the living room. There was broken glass and toppled over furniture. Blood stained the carpet and speckled the walls.

Silence blanketed the house for the rest of the night.

I'd never seen such an episode from my parents. I was seven years old.

2

Picture Perfect, Right?

I'M THE YOUNGEST OF four with two brothers and one sister. My parents were married at sixteen and seventeen years old, and our lives centered around the church. The church was our core foundation and the one constant in our lives. My dad was a leader in the church, so home life was routine, tight knit, and scripture based—with *a lot* of rules. He began his leadership journey in the choir then became a deacon, and he was ultimately ordained into leadership as an associate minister and ultimately a pastor.

He worked during the day and was a full-time pastor after work as well. My dad was a provider. We never lacked anything because he saw to it that we were taken care of. He made sure to surprise my mother with lots of gifts and special weekend dates. His biblical knowledge was strong, and he taught the Word well. He raised us on the Bible and taught us that God was the center of everything.

My dad is a hilarious guy and can find humor in many things. His humor was passed on as a dominant trait for my siblings and me along with his competitiveness. My mom brought balance, though. She has a quiet spirit and brings class and elegance into everything she does. She's a creative and can make something out of nothing with her eye for detail. I get my creative side from Mom. She was the homemaker, so she stayed home and took care of us.

My mom had no days off. I never witnessed a moment when she didn't care for her children or her husband, from a clean and perfectly decorated home to fixing us breakfast, lunch, and dinner and always making our plates. She did the laundry, ironed my dad's clothes, and prepared his bath water. The foundational values of home life were rooted into us through her. Her creativity and added touches made our house a home. I now see a lot of her traits in myself, though I felt we were opposites while growing up.

As the baby of the family, I shadowed my siblings, and though we were tightly knit, we all have unique personalities. I mastered each of them, depending on what the circumstance called for. My oldest brother, Dion, was the rebel, doing everything opposite of what our parents told him to do no matter the consequences. Many of the punishments we endured as kids were because of the things Dion had done. Our parents didn't want to make an example out of him alone, so they made sibling-shared examples. What I loved the most about Dion, though, was that he allowed me to do whatever I wanted and spoiled me to the fullest.

My second oldest brother, Tyler, was timid and quiet. He followed the rules because he saw Dion get caught for breaking them all the time. We affectionately called him "the innocent one" because it seemed he did everything right and never got into trouble. He was our parents' picture of perfection. He aggravated me because, while I was busy learning all the bad but fun things to do with Dion, Tyler was dull, boring, and by the book. He always wanted me to do right, but I was only concerned with having fun. Yet Tyler was about strategy. He focused on getting his work done and letting education be his ticket out of the house, and it worked. I was always granted permission to leave the house with him for various functions because he could be trusted.

My sister, Mallory, is my twin, although we're five years apart. It was always evident that we were the closest. Mallory has the personalities of both Dion and Tyler. She's an extroverted rebel with a huge dose of comedy. Her humor was like comfort food to us. She and I developed a great sense of humor together and created our own levels of fun. Mallory and I often got into trouble for talking too much, laughing too loudly, pulling pranks, or trying to get each other into trouble and watching it backfire. Mallory had a hustler's spirit. That spirit hadn't shown yet in Dion and Tyler. She was a natural-born sales woman, and she negotiated with our parents smoothly, earning her the privilege of having friends, going to events, and even driving their car the most. Unlike Tyler, who used education to get out of the house, Mallory was focused on working and grinding to get enough money of her own to get out. I admired Mallory so much. I took note of everything she did so I could mirror her when it was my time.

Then there's me. My personality is a combination of all my siblings, and I fine-tuned each of their traits and added finesse. I was a happy kid. I was drawn to my family and loved making new memories. We were like *The Cosby Show*. From the lectures to the fun moments, each episode was like a page from our family. Dion was Vanessa with a little bit of Theo. Tyler was Denise, Theo was Mallory, and I, of course, was Rudy.

I had a vivid imagination. I would turn my bedroom or our basement into my own fort by flipping over tables, hanging a sheet over the table legs, bringing in my pillows, blankets, and notebook to write. I could never go camping, so creating my own space was as close as it got. I often envisioned myself as a news anchor and would turn my desk into a news desk. I'd report on my own made-up stories to my imaginary television audience.

I had a natural hustle in me, too, as I would randomly create ways to get extra allowance money from my dad. They'd find me in the kitchen baking a cake, ready to sell it to my parents or getting my dad to agree to pay me more money to iron his handkerchiefs or church shirts.

I loved gospel choir music. One of my favorite things was listening to the crackling sound of the record while it spun on the record player, building up the anticipation of a great gospel song coming on. I would even line up my teddy bears to teach them parts and direct them while singing my solos. My love of writing formed at a young age, too. I wrote stories, journaled in my secret diary, and let my imagination go wild. I was also very emotional and sensitive as a young girl. When I was being disciplined, if my parents' tone was elevated, I would instantly cry. I hated conflict. I wanted to do whatever was needed to make things right, even if it meant being proactive.

Having older siblings, I naturally inherited a mature mentality. I heard all the time that I had an "old soul." I wasn't entertained by the things other kids my age thought were cool because I was listening to my older siblings' music, eavesdropping on their conversations, hanging out with their friends, wanting so badly to grow up.

Mallory and I were like two peas in a pod, and we both had a hustling spirit that, later in life, became my fuel to push past adversity. My fondest memories of my siblings are sneaking and listening to their music and having my own concerts. I would memorize dance routines from BET's Video Soul, bopping to Mary J. Blige's "Real Love" or Aaliyah's "One in a Million." I was the sibling who was most likely to drop an adlib rap in mid-conversation or start a freestyle karaoke battle. I was the talent of the family. I also developed a stigma for being a tomboy because I shadowed my brothers and dad. Everywhere they went, I went. Everything they did, I did. Their interests were my interests, from playing basketball in the backyard or park to watching Evander Holyfield and Mike Tyson boxing matches, even watching the NBA games, yelling at the TV in support of Michael Jordan, Scottie Pippen, and Dennis Rodman. I also shared their love for washing and detailing the family cars. We had a mini-vacuum, and vacuuming the cars was my duty along with wiping off the car wax. I also enjoyed cutting the grass and shoveling the snow.

My mom and I didn't have the best mother-daughter relationship when I was young. She was the judge, jury, and executioner if needed. I felt I always stayed in trouble more with Mom than with Dad. I just thought she didn't like me very much. I knew she loved me, but my mom wasn't the most loving, affectionate parent, maybe because she was a little girl overwhelmed. She had gone from being a young girl in her parents' home to being a full-time mother and wife at the age of 17. She didn't have a chance to be on her own. She had to be what and who my dad wanted her to be. It felt like she didn't have the time to show love through hugs, kisses, or girl talk. But when it came to household rules, she wasn't as strict as my dad, which made growing up with my mom bearable.

I didn't have a normal childhood because of Dad's strict rules. Mom did allow me to have three childhood friends with whom I went to school and could talk to, but it was our little secret. There were no play dates, no friends visiting, or sleepovers. Instead, there was a long list from my dad of what we couldn't do, who we couldn't talk to, not to mention, we couldn't interact with my mom's side of the family. We only spent holidays and weekends with my paternal grandparents.

My dad was a big disciplinarian who kept us sheltered. However, I can count on one hand how many times he ever actually gave me a spanking. All he had to do was raise his voice, and I cried. My tears were enough to show that I was remorseful and I got the point, no need for spankings.

I was a daddy's girl. My world revolved around him, and

he didn't—no, couldn't—do any wrong because he was a teddy bear in my eyes. I loved my dad. Some of my fondest daddy's girl memories are when my dad came home from work. I was the kid that always had to have a hug and kiss with occasional swing-in-the-air hugs from my dad. Sometimes, he would have some candy or a late-night Happy Meal just for me. I was the baby girl, and there were benefits to that. My mom understood because she was a daddy's girl, too, and out of her eleven siblings, she had been the one to receive perks like that also.

Bike riding was a favorite pastime for my dad and me. He had a special seat added to his bike just for me, and the faster he went, the more the adrenaline flowed for this young kid. The rides were followed by visits to Baskin Robbin's for strawberry ice cream. We would also go to the park, and he taught me how to swing.

My dad and I held a special bond with gospel music and old-school R&B. He'd teach me about the instrumentation before the lyrics. He would say, "Listen to that guitar. Hear those keys." His tutorials began with Stevie Wonder's harmonica tracks, "Fingertips" and "I Was Made to Love Her." He went on to teach me how to play Martha Reeves and the Vandellas' "My Baby Loves Me" on the piano. He then taught me how to play the drums to Aretha Franklin's "Respect" while he played the keyboard. We held mini-concerts while my mom laughed at us.

If it wasn't music, it was basketball. My dad had been an athlete in his younger years, and when he played with my brothers, I wanted in. Shockingly, he obliged and taught me the game. I was good, too. I was the only girl who could cross up a boy in middle and high school.

Outside of home life, we spent a great deal of our time at the church. If we weren't at church, we were at home getting Sunday School lessons drilled into us or memorizing Christmas or Easter program scripts while trying on homemade costumes. My mom was the church secretary and handled all things administrative like designing the weekly church bulletins. Church was the family business. I was bored with always having to go to church and flat out tired of doing the same thing over and over. We were at church Wednesday for Bible Study, Saturday for district meetings, all day Sunday, and by the time Monday hit, I was exhausted. And don't let there have been an all-week revival service with church service Monday through Friday. We'd come in from school, eat dinner, take a quick nap, and out the door we went.

We didn't have friends at church until our dad finally allowed us to befriend a select few who were there just as much as we were. The friendship was allowed mainly because their mom and grandmother played a big role at our church. Other than that, nothing.

My parents loved helping people, and people seemed to love them and us because we were their kids. Our church was small, so my dad handled a lot of the repairs, yard work, and overall maintenance. My parents taught us faithfulness in serving the church through their example.

With my dad as the pastor, there was no room for messing up. We were taught to respect our elders, say, "Yes, sir," and "No, ma'am," and not to speak unless spoken to. We were to be seen, not heard, and, "Don't you dare act out of character, or I'll come out the pulpit and spank you!" We were taught to always be concerned about what others said about us. If we didn't feel right, we had to fake it but never show it because our dad was watching us from the pulpit, his eyes piercing into our souls. We also learned the traditional bible stories day in and out. We were taught to fear God, that Jesus died for our sins and rose on the third day, and He's coming back again, keep the Ten Commandments, don't end up in hell, and scrutinize everyone who doesn't honor that list. Got it!

Church easily became a thing of routine, repetition, and perfection. We were being taught that perfection was the model because Christ was perfect, unaware that that type of striving pointed to an unreachable goal and disregarded the many examples of Christ having the most compassion for those who weren't picture perfect. I didn't know there was so much more to it. I also didn't think church life mattered that much; I just knew the basic overview and routine.

I found my place in the choir. That was no surprise since my dad's love for music was already embedded in me. The choir always gave me chills or moved me to tears, and I couldn't explain why. Something about how collectively beautiful the choir sounded always made me pay attention. Then I'd come home and direct my teddy bears to mirror the choir director I had watched hours earlier at church. My dad began teaching me how to sing because he sang as well.

Looking from the outside, we seemed like a perfectly average, happy, round-the-way family. But we were far from that.

3

Our New Normal

THOUGH THAT SATURDAY AFTERNOON was the first time I'd witnessed my dad hit my mom, I was later told it was a common occurrence. My dad had been abusing my mom since they were dating in high school, from telling her she couldn't accept her crown as prom queen to occasional slaps to the face during school hours. Through the years, his calculating manipulation and control became public. For years, the abuse was masked as a wife's servitude. The physical violence was hidden, but now the blinders were off. From that day forward, whenever my dad was having a bad day, he jumped on my mom, ultimately connecting the beating to his claim of her sleeping with his friend.

My dad began tracking the miles on her car and timing her when she went grocery shopping, to the mall, or whenever she left the house. She couldn't go anywhere alone; my siblings and I were made to go with her. If she was late, even because of traffic, he beat her and accused her of being out with her "boyfriend." It didn't matter if we were with her and could validate her story. He said she had brainwashed us, and our account of what happened was irrelevant.

My mom's screams and cries from the reoccurring beatings had grown so loud that they began reaching the ears of our next-door neighbors, giving confirmation to what may have previously been speculation. Our neighbors responded with concern and called the police. But our dad sternly instructed everyone to keep quiet. "What goes on in this house stays in this house!"

When the police finally arrived, my dad put his hand over my mom's mouth, squeezing her face tightly and smashing her lips together with his giant hand to muffle the sounds of her cries for help. With no lights on in the house, no one answering the door, and no sounds from inside, the police eventually left. I guess they thought it was a false alarm.

It happened countless times and, sadly, the neighbors eventually stopped calling.

There's nothing like the feelings that overcame me when I heard or saw my mom being abused. I felt extreme anxiousness and fear, and I was always on guard. I didn't know what the result would be. I didn't know if she'd make it out alive or what she was going to look like afterward. I dreaded seeing her and hesitated to approach her after my dad's rage ended. Bumps, bruises, cuts, and scrapes often left my mom's face disfigured. I constantly felt hopeless and worried for her, and the fact that I couldn't protect her made me feel powerless.

I had nightmares, sleepless nights, and occasional bed wetting, ramifications that caused a silent and deep pain within me, the type of pain that replayed my mom's abuse in my mind. The pain brought tears to my eyes at the most random moments, especially while watching TV shows or movies that even slightly or blatantly showed domestic violence scenes. Fear of the unknown tied my stomach into knots when I was at school because I was afraid of what I'd witness when I returned home.

However, through my silent pain, a fighter's spirit was rising within me. I was determined to get help for my mom. *Inspector Gadget* was one of my favorite cartoons, sparking my interest in gadgets and gizmos. The show was about an uncle and niece duo. The uncle was a detective solving cases, and he occasionally received unknown help from his tech-savvy, wise-beyond-her-years niece, Penny, and her dog, Brain. Following *Inspector Gadget's* lead and watching other shows like *Matlock*, I began trying to support my mom.

When fights broke out, I ran into the kitchen and grabbed the newly upgraded cordless phone to sneak into Mallory's room and call the police. Shortly after, I heard police sirens then the sound of them beating on the door. Oh, how my soul longed for their visits to be successful, but they never were. My dad had mastered the art of muzzling my mom and everyone else in the house through fear. There was a great unrest in my spirit that wanted to risk it all by screaming out so the police would hear me and force their way in, hoping that if they got into the house, they'd take my dad away, and my mom wouldn't hurt anymore. But the weighted fear overpowered my wishful thinking with doubt. *What if they don't take him away, or what if they do, but he comes back and kills us all?*

I found my parents' mini–recorder that they used for church services. My dad recorded his sermons on it. I took it to record my dad's frequent violent thrashings in the event the police made it inside or if my mom ever needed to go to court—evidence.

Since my dad was the pastor at the church, we were required to make weekly appearances as the happy family. However, the beatings left marks that makeup couldn't cover, and my mom was often unable to attend. We, however, were still required to go with smiles on our faces while our dad offered the same excuse: "My wife is out sick." His one-liner was the introduction to his sermon while he stared at us from the pulpit. With melancholy faces, we firmly held hands in the pew, trying hard to fight the tears that filled our eyes. We knew if one drop fell, it would indicate to the other congregants that his one-liner was far from the truth.

As the frequency of the beatings picked up, our school

attendance was impacted as well. My mom took care of our lunches, ironed our uniforms, and was still doing my hair. There were no backup options when she was recovering, so our dad made us start doing those things for ourselves. Though school was our only outlet, a piece of me hated leaving and being away from my mom. Thankfully, his work schedule changed to the day shift versus afternoons, so while we were at school, Mom was safe. The tradeoff was that he was now at home when we returned from school, which we hated.

Let's Go!

ONE AFTERNOON, AFTER CHANGING clothes from school and coming into the kitchen to fix my plate for dinner, I noticed my mom was on the phone and wearing a tense expression. As she held the phone to her ear, she gazed out the kitchen window that faced the major intersection behind our home just beyond our backyard. She observed the traffic intently, watching the cars drive past while listening to the other person on the phone.

"How is this part of being a wife?" she said. "How is this normal? This can't be normal. I never saw my dad abuse my mother or even yell at her. It's been happening since I was sixteen. Sixteen! I thought it would stop after all these years …"

I was frozen into shock as I eavesdropped on her conversation. My legs were heavy like I had on cement shoes; I just couldn't move to the next room.

"Tiffany get out of here!" she snapped.

I quickly grabbed my plate, moved out of the kitchen, and crept down a few stairs to continue listening while eating my food.

"Stop making him upset? Just be a good wife?" My mom said with indignation. "No, he needs to stop hitting me! I haven't

17

done anything. You know what, we aren't getting anywhere. Goodbye!"

I leaped over the remaining three steps and landed in the basement and jumped onto the couch like I'd been there the entire time.

On Friday, the following day, my oldest two siblings were home visiting. Dion had moved out and had his own place, and Tyler was staying on campus at college. We were downstairs watching *Out All Night*, laughing at one of Morris Chestnut's jokes, and I heard my mom go into the kitchen and slam the cordless phone onto the charger base. She stood at the top of the staircase and yelled down at us, "Hurry up and pack a bag. And do it quickly!"

We sat there on the couch looking around for a few seconds because we didn't understand what was happening.

"Didn't I say hurry up and pack? Let's go!"

We promptly followed her instructions.

We drove around for a while before ending up at a Red Roof Inn. We'd only taken one vacation as a family, and that was to Niagara Falls. Vacations weren't our thing. We were confined to our home or my paternal grandparents' house for weekend visits. Now, here we were in a compact room with two beds. It felt weird. I was over it and wanted to go home back to my bed.

We left the next day but not to go home. We ended up at Tyler's college friend's studio apartment. The apartment was heavily decorated with African décor and greeted us with the heavy smells of incense and smoke. My siblings and I didn't discuss how we'd ended up there or what our mom's plans were. As I looked around, I was curious about the paintings on the walls and the smell of incense surging through my nostrils. I was equally curious about the statues strategically placed around the apartment, and I wanted to meet the person who lived there. The apartment made me feel like I was in a museum. I'd never seen anything like it.

My mother argued with my dad for most of the day on her cell phone while we sat nearby quietly. We ended up going back home because my mom didn't have enough money to feed us all nor a plan to get us to school without uniforms.

The second time my mom left my dad was on another Friday afternoon. They started off arguing in their bedroom, and I was in the kitchen getting food after school. Mallory and I had an after-school ritual: get snacks then retreat to the basement for cartoons. I heard a loud bang. My dad had punched a hole in the wall, and shortly after, my mom came running out of their bedroom and grabbed me by my shirt on her way out the door.

"Let's go!" she said.

Who knew those words would trigger so much anxiety. We hopped into the car and flew out of the driveway as my dad ran out of the house trying to catch her. I cried uncontrollably.

"I want Mallory, I want Mallory!" I screamed.

"Shut up!" my mom shouted back at me.

It happened so fast. Mallory was already downstairs waiting for me to join her. I didn't understand why my mom only grabbed me. Why couldn't we have called and waited for Mallory to come? I found solace being near my sister; she was my constant, my safety and refuge in this new dysfunctional normalcy.

We never talked about how we felt about the abuse. There was just an implicit relief knowing the other person was there. Mom and I drove around for what seemed like hours before parking in an empty mall lot after she'd finally fed me Arby's. I had hoped to starve myself to the point of vomiting so she'd have no choice but to take me home, but my hunger wouldn't allow it.

I didn't understand why we had left home again. I understood the arguing, and I knew fighting was soon to follow, but we were gone again with no plan and, this time, without my sister. I was livid with my mom. I wanted to be back at home or, at the very least, be with my sister, and I couldn't have either. Since starving myself hadn't worked, I diverted to a backup plan—lashing out.

"I want to go home! I want to go home! I want to go home!" I yelled with uncontrollable tears. I cried until my sobs turned into gasps for air then hiccups.

My mom grew angry with me and finally decided we would go back home. But not without a warning. "Whatever happens to me is on you!"

I didn't get it, and I didn't care. The sweet internal chants of victory were too loud. I wiped my tears and smiled because we'd soon be back at home, and I'd be back in my own room.

When we returned home later that night, I got into my bed and grabbed my stuffed Mickey Mouse doll as the sounds of my dad beating my mom again tore through the walls of my bedroom. What seemed like sweet victory had quickly turned into a devastating loss. In my selfishness, I was clueless to the fact that I had sent my mom back like a lamb to the slaughter. I finally understood what her warning meant. Guilt flooded my heart as streams of tears flowed from my eyes. I felt sick to my stomach and cried all night.

The next day, my dad was called in to go to work. Once he left for work, I came out of my room to go into the basement. While walking past the bathroom, I glanced to my left to see my mom sitting at the edge of the tub running bath water to soak her bruised body. No one knew how to process the new normal in our home, but our hope was rooted in faith that one day it would end. During the times my dad had to work the dayshift, Mom initiated prayer circles every morning before school and again in the evening before my dad came home from work.

Our daily prayers were filled with pleas to God for the abuse to stop. We weren't equipped nor desired to accept this way of life. My siblings and I were often placed in the middle of our parents' fights. If we were with Dad, we had to appear to be on his side by not taking up for Mom, and we had to be against Dad if we were with Mom.

It was exhausting and invited isolation into my life. I desired to be alone. Isolation birthed an inability to develop social skills. I felt deserted, as if I were the only kid on the planet going through this. We couldn't have friends over because we had to hide the abuse. We never knew when the violence would rear its ugly head. God forbid a friend witnessed our dysfunction; the family image would be tarnished. We kept secrets from those closest to us and didn't trust adults with our truths to ensure nothing ever made its way back to our dad. We took on new responsibilities that required us to give up our role as children. We had to learn how to cook and handle the upkeep of the house while finding ways to comfort and console our mom.

At the age of nine, my life went down a road toward an uncertain future that wasn't on my map of destinations. In June 1994, my mom left my dad, and we didn't know where she went. It was a Friday afternoon, and Tyler was visiting home from college when our parents were fighting. Tyler, Mallory, and I were all downstairs when the screams drew closer and closer. As the screams approached, the back door swung open, and Mom sprinted out the door with my dad close behind. She jumped over our backyard fence into traffic on a busy main street, leaving her house shoes in the grass. Cars swerved and horns blew. My dad tried to catch her on foot but couldn't. He got into his car and sped away to find her. We all ran upstairs. Mallory looked out the back door. I looked out the kitchen window, and Tyler looked out the living room window.

"What do you think happened?" Mallory asked.

"I don't know, but this isn't good," said Tyler. "He's back! Hurry up and get back downstairs!"

My dad was unsuccessful at finding Mom and had come back, slamming the door furiously. "Y'all hurry up and get up these stairs and get in the car. Let's go!"

Confused and scared, we did as our dad instructed us. While walking to the car, I wondered, *What is he going to do to us?*

My dad drove around the neighborhood looking for my mom, going two miles an hour with his head on a swivel. He must have searched every nook and cranny twice, but we could find neither hide nor hair of my mother. It was like she had vanished. My dad didn't know if the police would come looking for him, so he took us to a hotel. Once he checked us in, he gave us directions.

"Y'all stay here! I'm going to look for your mother some more." He marched angrily toward the door.

We waited in silence for about ten minutes to ensure our dad was good and gone before talking amongst ourselves.

Mallory asked, "Where do you think Mom went?"

"No clue, but I hope she's okay," Tyler said. "She jumped into oncoming traffic from what I heard Dad say on the cellphone."

I sat there listening to their speculations and crying. I hoped and prayed she was safe. Tyler held me as I cried myself to sleep.

I awoke abruptly after hearing the door close, signaling my dad's return.

"I couldn't find your mother. I don't know where she is, but she left me. I'm going to take you all to your grandparents' house because I don't know if the police are going to come after me based on the lies your mom may tell them."

We didn't care about what he was saying; we were worried about our mom, wondering where on earth she could possibly be. We left the hotel, and he dropped us off at our grandparents' house before leaving again. He returned Saturday night to pick us up so we could make it to church, even though our mom was still missing. At church, he told the usual lie to the congregation, that our mom was at home sick.

The whole weekend went past without any word from her, and it began to take its toll. Later that Sunday afternoon, our frustrations and worries turned into fighting. Mallory and I got into a scuffle.

We were in the kitchen after church, fixing our plates when Mallory took the drumstick that I wanted.

"Mallory, that's the last leg, and you just snatched it out of my hand. Give it back and get the wing!" I whined.

"I don't care; it's mine now, punk," said Mallory.

I smacked Mallory's plate, causing her salad drenched with French dressing to stain her blouse. The rest of the food fell onto the floor.

"Oops," I said with a shocked expression.

Mallory tackled me onto the floor, and I gripped her face to get her off me.

Our dad came out of the bedroom and yelled at both of us. "I know y'all better get your butts off that floor before I give you something to cry about. Go to your rooms for the rest of the night before I spank you!"

We immediately stopped and departed for our rooms. I hopped into bed desperate for my mom, thinking about her as I stared at the ceiling. The fighting was a symptom of the bigger problem—our dad's behavior. Being forced to my room because of the fight brought about what seemed to be endless tears. Holding on tightly to my teddy bear, who had become my most trusted companion, I finally fell asleep.

I was awakened by Tyler. "Hey, get up. Daddy said you can come to the drug store with me."

I got dressed and followed Tyler to the car. The drive to the store was only ten minutes and a quiet one. When we pulled up and got out, he grabbed me to go with him to one of the payphones. It seemed odd. If we were going to the store, why were we stopping at a payphone? *You took me out of the house to stand here while you make calls?* I thought. I suppose I should have been grateful just to be out of the house.

"Hey, Ma," he said into the phone. "Yes, she's right here with me."

I was taken aback by his knowledge of her whereabouts, but my eyes lit up, and I smiled for the first time that weekend. A sigh of relief came, knowing she was safe. I'd never gone so long without hearing from her. I missed her. Tyler gave me the phone to talk to her.

"Hi, Mom! I miss you. Are you okay?" I asked.

"Yes, I'm okay, but we can't talk long because you must get home, but I'll see you later, okay? I love you," she said.

"This never happened. Don't tell Dad you talked to Mom," Tyler said.

"Sure. I can keep a secret."

Mom had said she would see me later, so I took that to mean she was coming home.

Our dad worked midnights, and as soon as he left for work at 10:30 p.m., Tyler rushed into my room.

"Get up. Put on some clothes and pack a bag."

"Huh, why?" I asked.

"I'm taking you to see Mom," Tyler responded while walking out of my room.

It seemed strange, but I obeyed. I didn't have the slightest clue of what was happening.

"Why isn't Mallory coming?" I asked.

"She doesn't want to come, and we don't have time to convince her. Let's go," said Tyler.

I thought I was going to see Mom for a couple of hours and come back home. We drove to the same store we had gone to earlier that day, but this time, the parking lot was empty and dark with only one other car, still running with the parking lights on. As we pulled up to the side of the car, I noticed my mom was sitting in the passenger seat with a lady I'd never seen before behind the wheel.

"Okay, let's go," said Tyler.

I grabbed my bag and greeted my mom with a hug. Seeing that she was okay made me happy.

Tyler hugged me. "I love you. See you later," Tyler said.

"Where are you going?" I asked.

He kissed me on the cheek. "You're staying with Mom. I have to go."

I was confused. Staying with Mom? Where was Mom even staying?

Mom opened the car door and forced me into the back seat. I realized the joke was on me. While I thought my mom would be returning home, the plan all along was for her to take me from my dad to be with her.

That Sunday would forever change the course of my life.

5

Why Me?

I INSTANTLY FELT BETRAYED. My heart was broken, and the tears fell uncontrollably. I wanted to go back home. If I couldn't go back home, at least I wanted Mallory with me. I only had the bare minimum of my belongings, which didn't even include my trusted teddy bear that I clutched in my scariest moments. It felt like I lived in a war zone, and my teddy bear provided comfort to help me sleep.

Both cars pulled off in opposite directions.

My mom said, "This is your aunt, and we're going to stay with her for a few days."

There were only two other aunts with whom I was familiar because they went to our church, but the other aunts I didn't recall. I cried the entire drive to my aunt's house, and the tears didn't stop when we arrived. This wasn't my home. I had only stayed at three locations: my house, my grandparents', and, occasionally, my brother's college dorm. I didn't want to be there. I didn't want to sleep or eat. I was sick and just wanted to go home.

To my surprise, I had a cousin there who was a year older than me. He did his best to try to make me feel comfortable through humor. Humor was always my comfort because that was something Mallory and I shared as siblings. I began to open up a little. With humor softening my discomfort, we played video games, and a new nightly routine formed. The few nights we were there, he and I watched *Tales from the Crypt*. Since I was never allowed to watch anything like that at home, I found a strange relief in rebelling against the rules.

After a couple of days, we left the first home to stay with another couple. They were friends of my brother, and their home was beautiful. They had a daughter who was also very sweet. She and I played together. I liked it there. I enjoyed the owners, the food was good, and I could feel myself relaxing. *Okay, maybe this isn't that bad*, I thought. The family was accommodating to my mom and me, but as soon as I got comfortable, later that evening, we were off to the next house.

We arrived at another couple's home, Dennis and Rebecca. They were friends of a friend of Tyler's who had heard about my mom's situation and wanted to be there for her. It was a big house in a suburban community. From the time I walked into their house, I loathed it.

Upon walking inside and being greeted, I got bad vibes. My spirit was unsettled, my stomach twisted into knots. The couple was pleasant and hospitable to my mom but very unfriendly to me. Their adopted niece, Marilyn, who was a year older than me, wasn't welcoming or hospitable either. Gentleness and sympathy laced their voices when they spoke to my mom, but everyone was seemingly irritated and emotionless when addressing me. They looked me up and down like I was a peasant. I felt like the stepchild in a Disney movie or the black-sheep cousin no one wanted around.

Every day in that house, anger built inside me, and feelings I never knew existed rose to the surface. I wanted to die most days. I didn't know what suicide was, but I hated waking up every morning with this family. They were empathetic about what my mom was going through and the pain she felt but called me a spoiled brat. On many occasions, I wanted to be with my mother only. My family was all I knew. We didn't socialize much or have family friends, so now that we had been scaled down to just my mom and me, she was all I wanted. When my mom wasn't around, they yelled at me and threatened to discipline me for the smallest things. I wasn't a bad kid at all. I wanted to leave. The first time I learned the word "hate" was at that house.

I'd never been treated that way. My mom was out of touch with what was going on, so bringing it up to her was pointless. She was just trying to survive and make a way for both of us. She had never worked before, but she took up jobs like house cleaning to try to provide for us. She was so strong, even in the face of extreme adversity, showing her hustler's spirit; she was willing to get it done no matter what.

When I tried to talk to her, she was too tired to listen or brushed it off as me just wanting to be home, which was true, but these people weren't good people. I didn't want to add additional stress on her, so I said nothing more. I quietly bottled my resentment and anger every day that we continued to stay in that house. I understood why we were in that predicament, but that didn't make it any better. I felt I was being punished for my parents' issues. Somehow, I was the one being mistreated and hit with the repercussions of circumstances I hadn't caused. Shouldn't the kid be treated with just as much empathy as the parent?

Tyler had given me his Walkman with some cassette tapes of songs we regularly listened to that he'd recorded from the radio. I began to fall in love with music even more, as it became my therapy. I started listening more to the words versus the instrumentation that my dad had originally taught me. It allowed me to tune out the madness of the house and be in my own world. I embraced my alone time and enjoyed the isolation.

There was a wooded area behind the house with plenty of trees and wildlife around. I made it my hideout, and I went there a lot to get away. I walked the trails and hiked alone. It was so peaceful. While I was in the woods, I discovered an unexpected peace in nature. I listened to good music, walked, sat in the clearings, and enjoyed being one with my surroundings. It was my temporary escape. It soothed the rage brewing in my soul and calmed my angry thoughts.

Marilyn was the antagonist in the house. When the adults weren't around, she'd frequently agitate the dragon that was inside me ready to spit fire.

"Your mom is homeless, but why do *you* have to live with us? I don't want you here, and stop playing with my toys," she'd say.

Every chance she got, she told me I was taking attention from her, and she didn't want me there. How was I taking attention from her when I was in trouble all the time? I didn't understand. I tried my hardest to ignore her and stay to myself, but the more I ignored her, the more she pushed my buttons. She'd use dishes and leave them around, blaming it on me, and the couple would complain to my mom about me.

"You think you're better than me? That's why your parents are getting a divorce!" she said.

All those boxing fights I'd watched with my dad and brothers paid off as I tapped into the inner fighter that was waiting to come out. My parents were off limits. Since I couldn't fight the adults, I began fighting their niece. The girl was a bully. What started out as simple arguments always ended up in fights.

I was never violent until I lived there. My brother and I wrestled a lot as kids, but we never fought. The techniques I had learned aided me in my attacks. I tried to take her head off each time. She never won a fight, so she was a tattletale each time, which only fed my rage. Fighting was my only defense.

The sweet little Tiffany who had been happy and jovial lost her smile. I was as dark as the home I was living in. The only benefit to living there was that the house was near Tyler's college campus. He checked on us a lot, and when he could, he stopped over to bring us food and money. There was a moment when Tyler was visiting us and I had a crying meltdown. I wanted to leave with him so badly.

"Tyler, please don't leave me. Please, take me with you. I don't want to be here; these people don't like me," I said.

"Tiff, I'm sorry. I can't. You have to stay here with Mom. I promise to come back early next week."

That wasn't enough for me. I jumped on a bike and tried chasing him down the driveway as he backed up and drove away. I peddled as fast as I could down the street, crying uncontrollably, begging him not to leave me. I became so overcome with emotion that I didn't pay attention and lost control, falling off the bike. I screamed, crying loudly until a neighbor and my mom came rushing down the street to carry me back to the house. I had scraped my knee, and it was gushing blood. Mom bandaged me up while giving me a lecture about being more careful and controlling my emotions. I still have the scar to this day. I was hurting inside and crying out for help, yet no one understood.

Toward the end of July, I was lashing out. I was angry all the time. I didn't want to play with Marilyn. I wanted to stay inside my assigned bedroom. I began talking back to my mom, becoming more vocal about my hatred of that house and how I was feeling about those people. My mom said I was out of control, but she couldn't see or understand what was happening inside of me. She couldn't see how this family was treating me. Being treated like a second-rate citizen and continuously reminded I wasn't wanted when I had my own family I couldn't be with was hell on earth to me. I missed Mallory the most. I missed my dad, too, but my sister was my everything.

On Mallory's birthday, my mom drove to a payphone so I could talk to her. My dad answered, and they argued for a while. Somehow, the church found out he was abusing my mom and that she left, so they forced him to step down. Eventually,

Mallory and I could talk to each other, but we only got a few words out.

"Hi, Mallory. Happy birthday!" I said with tears streaming down my face.

"Hey, Tiff. Thanks," she responded.

"I miss you so much."

"Miss you, too, Tiff." I heard her sniffles on the other end of the phone.

"All right, give me the phone back," my mom said.

"I love you," we said to each other.

The rage in my soul rose higher after that phone call.

I cried the entire drive back to the house and didn't talk to my mom. As soon as we arrived, I went into our room and cried myself to sleep. Only God knew how much I missed my sister, my house, my dad—my normal life.

We attended the church the couple attended. Naturally, I didn't like it, mainly because it was connected to them. Plus, I had been raised in a Baptist church, and this church was different. Baptist church services had devotion, which was comprised of two songs sang by deacons, followed by prayer. The choir marched in for a song and the congregation was welcomed into service. Announcements followed then the offering, another choir song, then the sermon. The new church felt more like a concert and had a much shorter service time. I was determined not to like it because I was rooted at the church I attended with my family. Accepting this church meant we wouldn't go back to the old. I didn't participate. I didn't sing. I didn't tell my neighbor anything when prompted nor did I engage during the sermon.

One Tuesday night, Rebecca sent me to the youth group while my mom just sat there like the cat had her tongue or something. Angry and rebellious, I refused to talk and pay attention. After youth group dismissed, I went to the sanctuary and came face to face with my mom as she was in mid-conversation with some other ladies, including Rebecca.

"I'm ready to go now," I said with an attitude I didn't attempt to hide from the ladies.

The women responded with looks of disapproval, and that was when things took a turn for the worse. The five women formed a tight circle around me. They placed oil on my head and put their hands on my head and shoulders.

"We're going to pray the demon out of you!" one of the women stated.

I was infuriated. My mom stood there crying without saying a word. I wanted to lash out and fight everyone. This was the church? This was how the church helped, by public humiliation and brushing off my trauma? Blaming it on a demon seemed to be their idea of a solution. I blamed my mother for allowing it.

When the prayer was over, I stormed off steaming mad and sat at the car waiting on my mom to join me. When she finally came so we could leave, we didn't discuss what had occurred. I refused to talk to her.

We stayed with that family for at least two more months, and things continued to go downhill. My attitude got worse and the fights increased. Marilyn and I got into another fight while my mom was at work. This time, Rebecca voiced her displeasure with me.

"I'm tired of you putting your hands on Marilyn. We don't tolerate that around here. You're very disrespectful, and we've had enough."

She pulled out a belt, and I ran away from her.

"Dennis, get her!" she yelled to her husband.

No man besides my dad was going to touch me. I ran into the room and locked myself in as they banged on the door nonstop.

"Open the door, Tiffany! I said, open the door! This behavior isn't tolerated here!"

I paced the floor, angry about how my mom had left me unprotected again. Enough was enough. I saw the phone lying on the table, and I called my dad. He answered after a couple of rings.

"Hello? Hello?"

I wanted to say something. I wanted to start a conversation. Just hearing my dad's voice gave my heart warmth. But instead of saying something, I hung up. I just wanted to scare them. But as soon as I hung up, the phone rang again, and the banging on the door dropped to a dead silence. I breathed a sigh of relief and cried myself to sleep.

I was awakened by my mom returning home from work early and pounding on the door. "Tiffany, open the door now!"

I knew that voice, and for her, I opened the door.

She slammed the door. "What did you do?" she yelled.

"What did I do? What did *they* do! They tried whooping me. Once again, Marilyn—"

"I don't care about that. How did your daddy know how to contact us?"

I was shocked into silence. *Oops!* "I only wanted to hear Dad's voice and scare them. You weren't here. I heard him say, 'Hello' a couple of times then I hung up."

My mom was furious. I watched her turn three shades of red.

"Well, because you wanted to call and hear his voice, he called back and heard Dennis, and now he's accusing me of leaving him to be with another man and having you here. We can't stay here. We have to leave because it's only a matter of time before he finds where we are. All because you wanted to hear his voice!"

My dad was able to call us back because of the newly invented caller ID. He had purchased it only to identify my mom's location the next time she called, and through my mistake, he'd succeeded. My mom wasn't dating Dennis, of course, but my dad didn't want to hear anything she had to say.

Selfishly, I was relieved that we could now leave. My mom

didn't feel safe not knowing what my dad's next move was, especially with the possibility of him knowing our location, and I didn't feel safe staying there with that couple and their niece. We moved shortly after.

6

On the Run ... Again

MY MOM AND I could've easily been the mother-daughter edition of Jay-Z and Beyonce's "On the Run" because life for us felt exactly like that. Tyler had a college roommate whose mom was a manager for an apartment complex in Ohio. She'd heard our story and wanted to help us. In September 1994, we moved into our very own two-bedroom townhouse. I was scared at first. This was a whole new beginning for us, just my mom and me.

I still missed my family and longed to return home to be with them. But the nervousness about our new beginning didn't outweigh how elated I was to be away from those horrible people in that house. Life seemed to be trending up for us. Mom was able to secure a job at a wedding boutique as the chief seamstress. We had a new home, and she also had a new car, a 1995 baby blue Tempo. My mom made sure I had a room and decorated it nicely. I had my own room and bed again. I was genuinely happy for the first time in months.

Mom enrolled me into a public school. It was an unfamiliar experience for me. Previously, I attended a predominately black private school from kindergarten through fourth grade. Now, in the fifth grade, I was attending a school that had a predominantly white student population. Changing learning environments was a culture shock for me and a significant transition. I cried on the first day. The teacher's taught with a radically different teaching style, and I had never been around other races. To make matters worse, the black kids, to whom I thought I could relate and hang out with, were the ones who bullied and teased me, especially while riding the bus to school in the morning. I hated riding that school bus.

My parents had always picked us up and dropped us off at school, so the experience was new. My mom still did my hair at ten years old. She'd styled it into sections with a traditional hair press and Shirley temple curls, slicked edges with a fair amount of Vaseline or Blue Magic grease where my hair was parted. The ponytail holders that matched my outfit were a dead giveaway that my mom still did my hair. Other girls my age wore their hair down with none of the bells and whistles.

I was teased daily on the way to school and when coming home. I had always been teased in school since kindergarten because I had dark lips. I was known as "charcoal lips," so being teased was nothing new. However, this form of teasing seemed crueler and more hurtful, mainly because I didn't know these kids. They called me "grease monkey" and "oily face," because my mom put so much grease in my hair. I held my anger in until one day, I snapped and fought the boys who bullied me every day. From then on, everyone noticed my temper and stayed away.

The teachers were friendly and warm. They knew about our circumstances and made sure to check in on me consistently. One teacher even encouraged me to play the flute, which I obliged and loved.

Mom was doing well. She loved her job at the wedding boutique, and since we had a car now, we were able to go places and do things together. We were finally doing all the things I'd been longing for, even spending mother and daughter time together. I still missed my family, but the yearning to be with them wasn't as bad. I felt safe again. I was learning a lot more than I'd learned at the private school back home, and I began loving my new home.

We still went to church with Dennis and Rebecca since the drive was only about forty-five minutes. One Sunday after the service, I had to leave with them and stay with them for a long time, which ultimately led to me having to spend the night. I was angry the whole time I was there and stayed to myself. My mom was nowhere to be found, and my anger was at an all-time high. Eventually, my anger turned into tears because I thought I had escaped them. I couldn't think of a justifiable reason for my mom making me stay with them. I tried not to sleep that night because of my stubbornness, but I ended up crying myself to sleep in a chair by the front door.

Somehow, my mom snuck into the house and was in the kitchen talking to Rebecca. Her voice was filled with tears.

"At nine fifty-four p.m., she took her last breath."

My mom had left me the day before because she received a call notifying her that my grandmother's health had taken a turn for the worse. I felt guilty as I listened to her cry. I walked into the kitchen to hug her. She stopped talking, wiped her face, and said her goodbyes so we could leave to go back to her family for planning.

The drive to my grandmother's house was a quiet one. When we arrived, we were surrounded by a lot of family members, including my mom's eleven siblings I'd never met. I didn't know until that moment I had so many aunts and uncles and a ton of cousins.

The night of the family hour, Tyler stormed into the house crying and took us into a room to tell us what happened.

"Mallory wanted to come to the family hour, but Daddy told her she couldn't come. She tried sneaking out, and Daddy jumped on Mallory!"

My mom was furious, pacing the room in disbelief. "He

hates me so much, he won't allow her to come. He's so spiteful! I'm going to go get her now!"

"No, you're not. Anything could happen to you or Mallory. We already have to bury our grandmother; we can't take the chance," Tyler said.

The funeral was the next day, and it was nerve wrecking and terrifying for me. Screams, cries, and pain saturated the room. Everything else was a blur. The day after the funeral was even harder. While all the adults were inside, I was outside with my cousins in the backyard. Some of my cousins were on top of the shed, and I was trying my best to jump up there and be included but to no avail.

"You're not a part of this family, anyway. Why don't you and your mom go back to where you came from?" one of the cousins said.

I was tired of trying to fit in where others didn't want me, so I walked to the front of the house to be away from them. I couldn't make out what was being said, but I heard yelling coming from the front part of the house. The adults were having a family meeting. I didn't want to know what was going on, so I sat on the curb.

Suddenly, my mom stormed out of the house. "Tiffany, let's go!"

She snatched open the car door and slammed it close before speeding off. She cried the whole hour-long drive home, and when we arrived, she still didn't talk. She stayed in her room crying in silence for two days, symptoms of her depression. My mom didn't cry much at the funeral, but she did during the following days. The grief had finally hit her.

In November 1994, my mom arranged to get Mallory the same way she'd gotten me, by sneaking her out while our dad was at work during the midnight hour. She was successful, and I was happy to see my sister. I hadn't seen her in over four months. I hugged her tightly for at least five minutes, crying tears of joy. We all drove back to Ohio, and it felt like all was right with the world.

My sister started attending a high school there, and it felt like we were a family again, even though my dad wasn't included. I walked around our apartment complex with confidence, chest puffed out with the biggest smile all because I had my sister walking by my side. Life was good, and we were creating new memories. However, on a late Friday night while we were all at home watching movies, Dion popped up to visit us.

"Hey, y'all. Look at my new car!" he said after gathering us outside.

He had a new 1995 two-door Ford Tempo. My mom had the same car, so I knew it was new, but I wondered how he'd gotten it.

"You and Mama have the same car now, nice! What happened to your other one?" I asked.

"It was my ex-girlfriends, but Daddy bought this one for me."

"Oh, okay. Congrats!"

We didn't think anything of it, so we walked back into the house and continued watching movies. Mom went back upstairs to her bedroom, and shortly after, the phone rang.

It was my dad.

My mom came storming down the stairs. "Who told your daddy where we are?"

It wasn't me this time. Mallory and I shrugged. I liked our new life, so I had no reason to tell, and Mallory had just joined us, so I knew she hadn't told.

"One of y'all said something! He knows where we live and how to contact me!" Mom said.

Dion finally fessed up. "I needed a car, so Daddy said he'd buy me one if I told him your location and contact info."

Mallory and I were shocked that Dion would sell out our mom for a car. There was a brief silence, then my mom jumped on Dion, punching him furiously. I had never seen her fight like that before.

Mallory pulled her off Dion.

"Get out of my house, and don't ever call me again!" she screamed at Dion.

He got up from the floor crying and left immediately while my mom retreated to her bedroom. My mom didn't speak to us about next steps, so we carried on with life as normal until one day, the phone rang, and I answered it.

"Well, hello there, Tiffany. How you doing?" my dad said.

"Hi, Daddy! It's so good to hear your voice."

"I miss you, you know that?"

"I miss you, too, Daddy."

I noticed my mom standing near me, and I froze. I passed the phone to her and walked away. It was all about survival, so my mom had no choice but to speak to him because she didn't know if he'd ever just pop up without us knowing.

My dad was back in the picture, and he wanted reconciliation. The phone calls came more frequently, and we spent the holidays together back in Michigan. They were taking it slow. My dad even came out to Ohio to visit us at our new place. It seemed as if we were normal again. He began mailing cards to me with sweet notes and sending money. I knew my mom loved him, but I didn't think she was ready to go back. She'd worked so hard to gain a new independence without the abuse.

As time passed and things seemed to be better again, my parents got back together in March 1995, and I was ecstatic. But Mallory wasn't. She was enraged.

We moved back to Michigan, back into our home. I think I kissed the ground. When I got to my room, I jumped on my bed multiple times and checked to see if everything was where I'd left it. I started attending my old school again and was reunited with my old friends. We were back!

The teachers at my old school knew what was going on, so

they were excited to have me in their classes again. Mallory, however, didn't return to the same school with me. She went to public school. Before having to leave my school and go on the run with my mom, my identity had been attached to my sister. Now, I was forced to come out of my shell.

My parents' marriage went back and forth. My mom went from leaving to coming back, to putting my dad out, then allowing him to come back home. The cycle continued from 1995 to the fall of 1997. My childhood had been stolen from me at the tender age of seven never to return. I was constantly caught up in my parents' struggle to maintain their marriage. They'd separate, but we always ended up back home again near the holidays. And like clockwork, as soon as it got warm outside, my dad started up again with the beatings. It was as if an alarm went off inside his head to remind him to be mean and cruel again. I didn't know what his trigger was. All I knew was the beatings were progressively getting worse.

One time, a couple of months after we had returned home, the beatings started again, and, once more, my mom left and took Mallory and me with her. Mallory was working two jobs while in high school, one job during the week and the other on the weekend. We went to pick her up from work at her weekday job, and we didn't return home. This time, we ended up living closer to home at another aunt's house with my cousin, Danielle, the one who had spearheaded the "You're not a part of the family" movement the day following my grandmother's funeral.

This new living arrangement was horrible. We stayed in a dank and swampy basement that was cold all the time. We slept on old couches that smelled of mildew, and if we weren't careful when we lay on the couch, we would land on top of a spring that could drill right into our spines. Danielle constantly provoked me to fight her. She went on and on with her cruel comments about me being a family outcast. She consistently mentioned my parents' situation as a joke the same way Marilyn had done.

When we were living in Ohio, I shared with Mallory that I was being bullied. I had also shared with her the things the kids would say. Mallory taught me how to cut back deeper and hit below the belt when folks tried to cut me with their words by saying things that would shut their whole world down. Along with a few fighting tricks, I was armed and ready for the next time they tried to come for me.

Her advice came in handy while living with Danielle. I didn't hold back any of my smart comments, and my aggression was elevated to an all-time high. Many times, my cousin tried to put me on front street while other cousins were over or while playing with the neighborhood kids. Anger and rage didn't cease to rise to the occasion.

My boy cousins were visiting one evening, and once again, Danielle thought it was okay to call me the b-word.

"Shut up b****!" she said.

"Who you talking to?" I replied.

"You, b****!"

I bent down to tie my shoe as she laughed then stood and gave her an uppercut to the lower jaw.

"Ooh!" everyone shouted.

My other cousins jumped up from the couch in amazement, ready to see more. I stood there with my fists balled, feeling vindicated like Laila Ali. As tears instantly filled Danielle's eyes, she regrouped herself and tried to come for me. Mallory jumped in to save her and told me to go upstairs.

Somehow, Mom got wind of the fight. She didn't like the fighter I was becoming, and Mallory had begun hanging out with her friends way too often. Feeling she was losing control, my mom decided to go back home.

We left my dad again in July 1996 and went back to my aunt's house. Things didn't get better with Danielle and me. The older I got, the more aggressive, violent, and unhinged I became. I fought at the slightest onset of conflict as if it were my only defense mechanism. The only way I knew how to express my anger was to confront her, a pattern I had developed from living with Dennis and Rebecca. Marilyn had bullied me nonstop, and I wasn't going to let it happen again. Thankfully, unlike the first time my mom left my dad, we were living ten minutes away from his house, and he had visitation.

Even though my dad was causing it, I felt like I was in the eye of the storm with him. I felt comfort. He never apologized for putting me in the middle, and he blamed my mom, but, somehow, it felt like home when I was with him. I knew what he'd done was wrong, but we had created and continued to create more memories together. We had gone shopping, eating, and to the park. We always had a natural bond through music, so we continued to build upon that bond. He exposed me to songs that communicated how he felt about my mom's absence in his life. "Distant Lover" by Marvin Gaye was one of them.

While my dad was schooling me on ballads and musicians' desperate pleas, he also slid in an occasional question or two—or three. He was using me for information. He wanted to know who my mom was talking to, where she was going, and what folks were saying about him. Since I was young and gullible, I gave him all the facts he needed. I was psychologically manipulated by my dad to view him as the provider of my material and emotional needs, to create a tainted view of my mother as the neglectful parent.

I confided in him about how my cousin was treating me.

"You need to start hitting her, no talking; just hit her," he advised.

"Well, I've been fighting her already," I said.

"Continue. We don't play that. Anyone who keeps disrespecting you or going against what you say, take their head off. Especially your mama's family."

One day, while Danielle and I were arguing, it turned physical again. Much like when we lived with Marilyn, while staying with my aunt, I was forced to do a lot of the chores Danielle never had to do. I was fed up. I'd finished washing the dishes, and she came into the kitchen with an empty bowl, dropping it into the sink.

"Why would you drop this in the sink when you see that I'm done? Wash it!" I demanded.

"I don't have to do anything. That's why you have to!"

"I'm not doing anything because you suck. Lazy bastard. You never have to clean up anything!"

"That's why your parents are getting a divorce!" she said while walking back to her room.

I desperately wanted my parents' marriage to work, so I wasn't accepting any snide comments about them. I threw the dish towel on the counter and ran after her, pushing her into the wall and pulling her hair. My mom was in my aunt's bedroom talking to her when she ran out and tried to get in the middle. The fight escalated as my mom tried to intervene, and Danielle accidentally hit her in the face. My rage took over. I pushed my mom out of the way and proceeded to wrap Danielle's hair around my hand, slamming her onto the ground, putting her in a headlock. My mom grabbed me from behind, and her mom grabbed her.

My mom pushed me outside, hitting me and yelling at me. "Tiffany, you are out of control! Stop it! Stop it, now!"

I wasn't trying to hear it. Being violent allowed me to release all the internal pain I was feeling.

~~~

After a tumultuous summer, my mother moved us back home. She was sick of me and my fighting, and Mallory was hanging out all the time, not listening to her, either. I was excited to go home. There was a catch, though: My dad had to move out. That didn't disappoint me because I got to be in my own house and bed again.

It was much better than sleeping on a couch in a swampy, cold basement at my aunt's house and sharing a bathroom the size of a shoebox. With my dad gone, a lot of things changed. Mom wasn't as strict and allowed both Mallory and me leeway to provide some balance. She allowed me to go out with my best friend, and she let her come over. I was also able to ride my bike throughout the neighborhood. My dad only allowed me to ride the bike up and down the driveway and on the sidewalk in front of the house. She let me have more freedom to dress my age instead of wearing skirts to my ankles. Mallory even hung out with her friends more as well.

I was becoming slightly interested in boys. Mallory was a little player, and I tried to mirror her and had a few school crushes. I ended up only having phone boyfriends because I couldn't see them in person, so the crushes never amounted to anything serious. Then my parents got back together later in 1996, and she let my dad come back home—again.

Everything was cool until March 1997, when the drama started again. I was home alone with the music blasting, dancing in the living room to Biggie's new release "Hypnotize" when I heard the garage open. I ran to the kitchen to look through the blinds facing the garage, and, sure enough, it was them.

Oh, snap! Let me hurry up and cut this off. I changed the radio station back to the Christian station they'd had it on and ran downstairs to watch TV.

My parents were home early from the church banquet they'd attended. From what I overheard, a guy sitting at the table with my parents had poured my mom some coffee, and my dad went off on the man. He didn't jump on him, but on the car ride home, he berated my mom. Somehow, a simple gesture of pouring coffee was my mom's fault, and the arguing continued when they got back. Thankfully, he didn't hit her that time, but we were all on eggshells.

Tyler's college graduation was the following month. There was a lot of tension at the onset of the day, and I didn't know why. From the time we took pictures at the beginning of the ceremony until after, something was brewing. The drama began when we were taking photos of Tyler. Tyler's row was called to go line up for their name to be called, so we ran down to get pictures of him walking across the stage.

As we stood, excited for Tyler, I heard my dad's voice. "You don't wanna test me; you don't know me. You better gone somewhere now. I don't play games."

Something had occurred, and my dad was exchanging words with the photographer, ready to fight him. Mallory and I looked at each other, confused. Tyler's name was called, and he walked across the stage, degree in hand. We took pictures and immediately went back to our seats. It was hard to be excited for him when we were terrified of what Daddy was about to do.

We had another car ride home filled with arguments, leading me to confining myself in my room as they continued at home. I started to realize a pattern. Whenever we attended an event outside the house, my dad always introduced conflict and ruined it. I still didn't know how to process these occurrences. I only prayed we didn't have to leave again.

A few months later, it was Mallory's high school graduation. My dad didn't cut up until after the ceremony this time. Apparently, some man from their old high school was looking at my mom. Another graduation ruined. Another family event destroyed. A few weeks later, my dad started hitting my mom again, and she put him out. I was so grateful that we didn't have to leave that time. I was over it and becoming numb.

Toward the end of May 1997, I found myself in serious trouble at the Christian middle school I was attending. I called my teacher a b-word in front of the class because she had taken my *Vibe* magazine with Sean "P. Diddy" Combs and Biggie on the cover. P. Diddy was my childhood crush. Unbeknownst to me, the teacher called her sister, who came up to the school to confront me.

As I sat at my desk fuming, I felt a tap on my back.

As I turned around, her sister said, "So you called my sister a b-word?"

"Who are you?"

"Answer the question."

I refused to back down from a fight. I got up from my desk with even more aggression. "I'm calling *you* a b-word now."

The class was in an uproar. My best friend rushed to separate me from the woman while other teachers came into the classroom. They quickly ushered me to the principal's office.

"Tiffany, you can't leave until your parents come and pick you up," the principal said.

"That won't work. My sister picks me up from school. You can talk to her."

"What did I say? You aren't going anywhere!"

My best friend came in and asked if I was okay. I told her what was happening. Shortly after, Mallory came into the office. "What's the problem?" she asked.

The principal repeated what she'd told me.

"I don't give a d*mn what you said. I'm her transportation for our parents. She's leaving with me," Mallory said.

The principal refused to let me go, but before Mallory could form another word to continue the cuss-out session, my best friend's mom walked in.

"I don't know what y'all got going on here, but this baby is leaving with her sister. From what I was told, everyone is wrong in this situation. I'm her parent in their absence."

My bestie and her mom knew the details of my home life, so they knew the reason my dad couldn't be called up there, and

Mallory had the car, which prevented my mom from picking me up.

My heart smiled as she told me to grab my things and come with her. Victory!

Not so much ...

They expelled me from school and threatened not to pass me to the eighth grade. My academic performance had nothing to do with the verbal altercation with the teacher and her family, so they had no valid reason to hold me back.

After a month, my mom let my dad return home from his parents' house to handle the situation. Yes, I was wrong, but things were escalated by the teacher when she'd called her sister, and my parents agreed. My dad had a relationship with the elder who had started the school and paid the school a visit to alert him to what was happening with his staff. The elder apologized and allowed me to home school for the last two weeks of the semester without my parents having to pay tuition for that month. We received a letter after the school year ended informing us that the school was closing. The shutdown afforded me the opportunity to go to a charter school for my eighth grade year, which was as close as I was going to get to a public school.

Dion moved back home. He was expecting his first baby in a couple of months, the first grandbaby for our parents and my first niece. The new addition proved to be good for the family dynamics and ushered us into a new chapter. My parents seemed to be getting back to the days of no fighting. They still argued, but there was no violence. My dad kept it cool.

I settled into my new school. My circle began to grow larger. Outside influences became stronger, and I began looking to my associates at my new school as my model for normalcy. They didn't know about my dysfunctional home life, but I'd listen to stories about their social activities, and those things became much more appealing to me.

7

Let's Talk About Sex ... or Not

In 1999, I was transitioning from my tomboy phase and wanted to dress and be more girlie, but my dad wasn't having it. I played basketball in junior high, but as my body was developing, I had to stop because my sports bra could be seen through my jersey. I was so thankful for the circle of friends I had come to know. They brought me clothes to change into during school hours. I came to school in one outfit, changed into another one, and was back into my regular clothes by the time my dad or mom picked me up.

My parents were strict about our grades, so doing my work and getting good grades wasn't an issue. I was a master at doing the right things and being sneaky about the wrong things. I began sneaking and having more conversations with guys on the phone by making my parents believe I was talking to girls. I informed the guys of the hang-up rule. I would conveniently fail to inform my parents when we had half days so I could sneak away with friends to be around boys. I was paranoid about even contemplating the next step, but I thought I was smooth. I quoted song lyrics and mesmerized them to get into their heads.

I was so good that they wanted more, but I kept them at bay. It seemed like I had more guys after me when they found out I was a virgin. I became a conquest to them.

I wasn't getting the attention at home, so the attention from the boys felt nice. My best friend and I were masters at secretly dating and having our own "hang-up code." If someone picked up the phone, we didn't say a word. We just knew to hang up without saying bye. She was my confidant for all things, my right hand.

Although the thought of sex terrified me, I wanted to experience the feelings I'd heard about in the songs. It sounded so romantic, like I'd be whisked off to paradise with the love of my life. How I longed for an escape from the madness at home. My family didn't talk about sex. We were commanded not to do it. Period. My friends had either lost their virginity, or they were on the way to losing it. I was the only one in the circle who hadn't dabbled in that arena yet. My circle told me that, at fifteen, we were at the socially acceptable age to do it, and I was too sheltered. I figured they were right; what did I know?

I learned sexual talk and behavior from friends, family, movies, and music. As my sphere of the outside world increased, I had access to pornography, magazines, and movies along with the opportunity to listen to some of my brothers' friends and male friends as they held discussions about it. Sex was everywhere, especially in the oversexualized love songs that planted seeds in my spirit and painted a mirage of a false reality.

The movie *Love & Basketball* highlighted hopeless love and a gentleness when a girl loses her virginity, romanticized by the song, "This Woman's Work" by Maxwell. My boyfriend lived up the street from me. We had gone to middle school together and met up at the local drug store while in high school and began dating. I confided in him about the terrors in my house and started feeling like he genuinely loved me.

I maintained my virginity until June 2000, a few months

shy of my sixteenth birthday. I was over his house, and we were watching movies. He made the moves, and I thought maybe this was my *Love & Basketball* moment.

It was whack, and it was quick. Worse decision ever.

I fell for a knucklehead and gave in to peer pressure. It was nothing like the movies. I was disappointed I had given my virginity up. As I spoke to other girlfriends about the horrible experience, they encouraged me to continue and promised it would get better the more I did it.

Having older siblings worked to my advantage. From them, I learned to lie about my activities and whereabouts when I was really sneaking off to be with my friends or boyfriend. Mallory was still my twin, but Tyler was my means of transportation, and my parents trusted me with him without question. However, when I really wanted to do something and didn't feel like lying to achieve my goal, I could always count on Dion. He never asked any questions. He lived closest to our house, so every time my parents argued and the climate sucked at home, all I had to do was call Dion and tell him to drop me off at a friend's house.

I began escaping my parents' reality by having sex. I didn't even enjoy it. It was, sadly, just something to do. I thought it was love and what people in love did, so I obliged to keep my boyfriend.

I thought my boyfriend loved me until I saw him out with another girl when I was out shopping with my mom. Rage consumed me, yet I couldn't let it out. As soon as I got home, I called Dion to take me to his house. I grabbed my mom's sewing scissors and put them in my pocket. I was determined to show him I wasn't the one to be played with. I banged on the door repeatedly, and his mom opened it. I held the scissors behind my back and asked if he was home. He wasn't. God was protecting me from me.

From then on, I decided that I, too, would become a player. If guys could do it, I could, too. I broke up with him and played it cool. There was a new guy at school I was eyeing. He was older, a smooth talker, and experienced in the bedroom from what I'd heard during the girl chats in class. I took him on as a challenge and won. The more sex I had, the more my temperament changed. It became my addiction.

Tyler had a best friend named Karen whom we hung out with a lot. Karen had become aware of my flippant attitude and remarks and my impatience and tantrums when I couldn't leave the house. I acted out toward my parents and siblings when they pushed my buttons. One day, while over Karen's house, I was trying my hardest to get Tyler to let me invite my boyfriend over, but Tyler wasn't having it, and I started pouting.

Karen was in the kitchen cooking when she suddenly came around the corner and yelled, "Oh, she's having sex! You don't try that hard to get someone to come over and react like that unless you're getting it in!"

I was speechless.

Tyler turned and looked at me. "Have you had sex yet?"

I couldn't lie to Tyler. "Yes," I said.

"When and how?"

"Last summer, and Dion took me over his house."

Karen laughed, and Tyler rolled his eyes. "Typical Dion," he said.

Karen stopped cooking mid-meal and ordered a pizza instead to give me "the talk" and get the details about my boyfriend. I'd never been given the sex talk, so Karen led the conversation and was adamant that I use protection each time. Karen also cautioned me about guys and how, for most boys out there, it's their mission to have sex with girls and keep it moving. She warned me to be careful and not give it up to everyone.

Shortly after, my new boyfriend dumped me. He was too experienced, out of my league, and he had a baby on the way. I wasn't ready to handle the reality of being dumped and cheated on *again*. I wondered if I would always be cheated on. I couldn't have regular dates and conversations outside of school because of my parents' rules. I resented them for the rules, yet my inexperience justified their reasons. My parents were trying to save me from the grief of heartbreak from having sex at an early age.

In June 2000, my dad began hitting my mom again. One afternoon, my parents were fighting downstairs, and I was upstairs listening from my room. It was pointless to call the police because they never could get through, so I just prayed it would stop as usual. However, this time was different.

I heard a loud noise followed by my dad's scream and my mother running up the stairs from the basement and opening the kitchen drawer. I ran out of my room and through the living room into the kitchen to see the drawer still open. I started to run downstairs to see if my dad was okay but immediately stopped at the top of the basement steps.

My mother was sitting at the top of the stairs with a butcher knife in her hand.

"Go back to your room!" she ordered.

I couldn't move, though. As I stood behind my mom and looked down, I saw my dad lying at the bottom of the stairs screaming and crying in pain.

"He wanna try to hit me again, I got something for him. I'm not going to keep taking it. I kicked him in the groin, and he fell. And before he tried to come after me again, I snatched the door off the hinges and slammed it down on his knees. Now, like I said, go back to your room!" she yelled.

I turned around and softly grabbed the cordless phone off the base and ran to my room.

I called Tyler. "Tyler! Mama and Daddy started fighting again, and Mama ripped the door off and slammed it on Daddy. Now she's sitting at the top of the stairs with a butcher knife waiting for him to come up the stairs after her. I think she's going to kill Daddy."

"Stay in your room. Close the door and pray."

Tyler had nothing else to say. What could he say? I wasn't going to call the police on my mom. My dad had hit her all these years without anything happening to him, so I wasn't about to call on her when I knew she was defending herself.

A couple of hours passed, and my mom came into my room. "Get dressed. We're going to the hospital."

Huh? I thought. All these years he'd beat her up, and we never went to the hospital. *Did she stab him while I was in my room?* I failed to comprehend.

My dad could barely walk and was bleeding. Apparently, splinters from the door had gotten through his clothes and cut him deeply. The ride to the hospital was a quiet one, and I was curious about how this was going to work out. I hated to see my dad in pain, but I was proud of my mom. Finally.

We checked him into ER, and the nurse asked, "What happened?"

My heart pounded because I didn't know how my mom was going to explain this. What was my dad going to say?

"His knees gave out, and he fell down the stairs," my mom quickly responded.

Oh, snap! How'd she come up with that so quickly? I thought.

The nurse bought it and treated him accordingly.

Within a few hours and after some pain meds, Dad was discharged, and we were heading home. Just like that, they went back to normal. But little did I know, after that incident, my mom began devising a plan to leave again.

While I was proud of my mom's behavior, she wasn't. She believed my dad was either going to kill her, or she was going to kill him. It was fight or flight, and she chose to fly.

March 2001 was set-it-off month. Mom picked me up from school and said we were leaving and taking everything. I couldn't believe it; out of all the times we'd left, this was the first time my mom had a plan. The only thing I didn't know was where we were going. It was kind of exciting, like we were doing a hit on our own house like the movie *Ocean's Eleven*. We took everything except the beds, couches, TVs, and my dad's stuff. My mom kept the new car my dad had purchased her, a 2001 Lincoln LS.

I called my guy friends from school to help us out so we could cover more ground. They agreed, and we began moving as soon as I got out of school. We finished an hour before my dad came back from work at eleven p.m. that evening. We spent the night at Mallory's house because we knew our dad would be on the prowl, but this was the last place he would come. My mom even cleaned out the savings in the bank account they shared so she could take care of us.

Eventually, we ended up living with Tyler in his one-bedroom apartment because it was closest to my high school. It was super tight, but, by this time, he'd become my favorite sibling, so I was excited. He, however, was not happy. He was there, though, and I appreciated that.

Tyler endured a lot for us. His apartment was already tight, but he still moved a twin bed in so I could have somewhere to sleep. He was my mom's constant support, giving her money when she didn't have it and providing her alibis. He shared his connections for our betterment and provided food and shelter, co-parenting with my mom. He was the responsible one, stretching himself and sacrificing his social life to always be there for us and help us. My childhood was taken from me, but I didn't understand that my parents' drama had snatched away his early adulthood. Tyler had been in the middle of my parents' madness ever since he'd started college.

He took me to campus functions with him and introduced me to his friends and social network, and even when he began a career in teaching, he had me right there in his classroom. These interactions not only helped me learn, but they also helped me mature a lot faster.

Tyler was my voice of reason throughout high school. My mom was going through so much, and our only communication was through arguments. She was already fussy, but now, if I wanted to go hang out with friends, it was an argument because she wanted me to sit in the house.

I hated staying home and being around her. All she did was talk about my dad and their arguments or cry. I didn't want to see that or be around that, yet she scolded me whenever I tried to leave. Everything was an issue when it didn't have to be. Tyler kept me sane.

Since Tyler knew I had boyfriends and a thriving social life, he served as my getaway and offered me outlets and guidance along with Karen. They coached me to be safe and take care of myself as a young woman to ensure I didn't go down the wrong path. Their plan was smart. They stayed close enough to watch me because no one else was paying attention. They also were my safe place for me to vent and just be myself. High school was a lot more fun because of them.

My parents' separation opened another door of opportunity for me. I took driver's training with Tyler's help, and he often let me use his car to hang with friends. He would also take me to see our dad, but those visits were not the highlight of my day; they were depressing. The house was a mess. My dad had slimmed down and looked like he hadn't eaten in weeks. But he still had old habits. He bribed me by giving me money on each visit, and we scheduled days for him to bring me lunch at school. He worked afternoons, and I had a key to the house, so I made his place my hangout spot. I would go over there and have my friends come over like it was my own. I hung out with my friends during the summer and weekends, and I was having a lot of sex, using it to relieve stress from the constant arguments between my mom and me. Despite the dysfunction, I felt like I was having a pretty normal life, and my smile was a lot bigger.

While having a blast building my social life, I still worked hard leading up to my senior year. The classes that sparked my interest the most were psychology, English, creative arts, and, surprisingly, Spanish. Any class that allowed me to create, analyze behavior, or write had my full attention. In Spanish class, the teacher required us to create our own magazines to capture the details of the class and bring the topics we discussed to life. I loved creating the front and back cover art and writing various articles about current events, including fashion and lifestyle tips. I received a perfect grade each time.

Tyler had a close friend named Greg Harden, who is a life coach, athletic counselor for The University of Michigan, motivational speaker, and executive consultant. He's best known for his work with six-time Super Bowl champion quarterback Tom Brady and working with Heisman Trophy winner and Super Bowl MVP Desmond Howard. He also worked with Olympic gold medalist Michael Phelps. I'd met Greg earlier in my life through Tyler, when my mom had left my dad before, while we were living with Dennis and Rebecca, yet I didn't have conversations with him. I was suspicious of any man who wasn't my father.

Tyler brought me around him through monthly lunches or campus activities. It was through those outings I discovered he was a counselor, and he was observing my behavior and interactions. After his observations, he would frequently drop nuggets of wisdom, advising me on the game of life and how to positively adapt instead of the negativity he had observed. I desired to attend his motivational speaking seminars with Tyler, and Tyler obliged. I became a sponge, soaking up all the knowledge and tips he gave while taking notes and translating them to my understanding, sending them to him as recap summaries.

"You're a writing fool. You took all of this from my seminar?" he said.

"Yes."

"You really have a gift for writing."

He was the first one to tell me that and look past the negativity that everyone else saw, uncovering a talent beneath the surface. I slowly began to trust him and his voice, so when he gave me my first impromptu coaching session, I didn't resist.

"No one can hear the message of what you're truly saying through your behavior. The outside world isn't your family; they don't care. You must learn how to change and adapt. I understand why you're so angry. That's why you have so much bottled-up bitterness. You're this way for a reason. It's a protective mechanism. You're protecting yourself by being cold, withdrawn, and non-trusting because it keeps you sane in an insane world. I'm amazed by your capacity to build a bunker around your mind, heart, and soul to minimize the effect everyone has on you. I'm impressed by the fact that you are so clear on who you are and who you aren't. You're running your life, and no one can mess with you. But I caution you to still be on alert but not push everyone away because there's some folks you may need as you go through this journey of life."

I'd never allowed anyone to pour wisdom into me, and I never wanted to follow anyone's advice. Yet, I was impressed with his observations, and I was open to hear more. I even made some of the adjustments he recommended.

"The best revenge is success," he advised. "Someone in the family has to say, 'It stops with me.' Out of everyone in your family, I believe you're going to be the one who gets it and sees outside of the box. You're going to make it. Just stay focused and be open to getting some counseling."

He became my mentor and like a godfather to me as I embraced his words of wisdom. Not only did he see the real me, he believed in me, which was a first and meant a lot coming from someone with his background. I began to share with him projects I worked on at school, and he encouraged me to develop my writing gift. He recommended that I apply for an internship during the summer to not only help me get away from home life, but also expose me to new environments.

My love for creating and writing led to my aspirations for a career in journalism and starting my own magazine. I applied for internships with the *Detroit Free Press*, which opened doors for me during the summers. I didn't get the internship, but during the summers of my tenth and eleventh grade school years, the *Free Press* paid for me to go to journalism camps. I went to a camp at Central Michigan University in my tenth grade year and Michigan State University in eleventh grade. Both were excellent experiences.

I was on an educational high; however, toward the end of August 2001, something strange happened. I felt nauseated during random times of the day. The nausea continued every morning for three days, and I knew something wasn't right. I called a friend.

"Hey, I feel strange. I've been nauseated every morning for the past three days," I said.

"When was the last time you had a period?" she asked.

"Umm ... middle of July."

It was now the end of August.

"You're pregnant, Tiff!"

"No, no way! I can't be. That's not possible."

"Go to the store and get a pregnancy test immediately."

We hung up, and I was in disbelief. I was just two weeks away from starting my senior year in high school. I couldn't be pregnant. Senior year was supposed to be the most enjoyable time of my life.

I walked to the store five minutes from Tyler's house and got a test. My worst fear was confirmed. I thought about how this could have happened, and I knew exactly how I'd gotten pregnant.

During the summer, after I returned from journalism camp, I had sex with my new twenty-five-year-old boyfriend, Pierre.

59

I met him as soon as school let out for the summer at a record store. He pulled up in my favorite car, a Pontiac Grand Am. He looked like a muscular version of the rapper Young Joc. He flirted and quickly asked me for my number, and I obliged. I didn't know his age, and I didn't ask because he didn't look older. He called me the same night to schedule a date.

Wow, a date! I thought. I'd never been on a date, and since my parents were separated, I could go.

We went on a series of dates, and one day before I left for camp, he picked me up from my friend April's house. Her brother was sitting on the porch with us when he pulled up, and he knew my boyfriend.

"Aye, what up, Pierre?" he said.

April and I looked at each other, surprised they knew each other. I smiled because that must've meant he was a good dude.

"All right, see y'all later!" I said while getting into the car.

April texted soon after: *Girl, did you know he's 25?*

Me: *Umm, no, we haven't discussed age.*

April: *Well, he hangs with my brother all the time.*

To my surprise, as soon as I received her text message, Pierre asked me my age. "So, you hang with Chris's sister? How old are you?"

"I'll be eighteen in a few months," I said, which was far from the truth. I would be turning seventeen in a few months.

"Oh, okay."

We didn't speak about it anymore. He was a gentleman. We went to the movies, dinner, and when we returned, he gave me a kiss good night, and that was it.

Then I went away for journalism camp. I missed him a lot while I was gone, and we talked frequently on the phone. When I returned, he said he was glad to see me, and after dinner, he wanted to bring me back to his place for movies. I agreed, and within ten minutes of the movie starting, he began kissing me and sliding his hand up my dress. I was a little hesitant because I knew his age, but because he was older, I felt I had no choice.

I had used protection with all my exes, but Pierre gave me the "I love you. We don't need a condom" speech, and I gave in. In my mind, this was the perfect *Love & Basketball* love scene setup. But they had used a condom—stupid me.

Now, here we were a month later, and I was pregnant. I knew my parents would kill me if I told them, and I couldn't bring a child into our toxic environment.

I had to tell Pierre. I had been avoiding him ever since I found out. I called him on Labor Day 2001.

"Hey, how are you?" I said.

"I'm cool. So why you start going MIA?"

"Well, I'm pregnant and I've been figuring out how to tell you."

"You sure?"

"Yes, I took a test, and I missed my period for August."

"I'm going to take you to Planned Parenthood to confirm," he said.

"Okay, and when they confirm, then what?"

"You're not keeping it. That's not an option; you're getting an abortion."

I'd never heard of abortions. I had no clue what to do or who to talk to.

I turned to a friend for her opinion. Naïve and unaware that I was receiving non-biblical advice, she told me to have an abortion as well, so I was convinced it was the right thing to do.

"You know your parents and family can't handle anymore surprises. You'll be adding more stress to your mom. Your future is set before you. It's perfectly okay; people have abortions all the time," she said.

I was still on the fence, so I spoke to others, hoping someone would give me other options to consider. They all confirmed that it was normal and even they'd had multiple abortions. Although

I wasn't perfect by a longshot, I had grown up with Christian values; however, I never considered asking another Christian for advice. Maybe things would have turned out differently.

Without any support from my so-called boyfriend and everyone encouraging the abortion, I allowed my friend to mentally prepare me for the process.

We set an evening appointment, and Pierre took me to Planned Parenthood where they confirmed my pregnancy. They gave me the options of adoption, keeping the baby, or having an abortion. Without blinking, Pierre said, "We'll be having an abortion."

I was mute as the nurse told us it would cost $400. He said, "No problem" and asked to continue with scheduling.

The nurse advised that, due to my age, I had to go to court and plead my case to a judge, explaining why I wanted to have an abortion without my parents' knowledge. My court date was the following week, and I had to skip school to attend the hearing. My explanation to the judge echoed my friend's reasoning—my family's dysfunction, my college acceptance, and having no support to care for the child. Upon the judge's approval, I proceeded with the abortion appointment.

I felt like crap because I had to kill my baby growing inside me, and I was physically sick during my pregnancy. I never vomited, but I was severely nauseated all the time and had to hide it from my mom and Tyler in the mornings, when it hit me the hardest. I couldn't eat my favorite foods because they triggered my nausea. I could only eat the foods Pierre ate. I cried a lot. Parts of me wanted to keep the baby, and I wondered what it would be like to have it. I had three nieces and one nephew, so I knew the basics of caring for a baby, but my future and thoughts of losing what I'd worked so hard for in academics haunted me. I tittered with my decision: one minute, yes, the other minute, no.

I had a 3.8 GPA, I was on the National Honor Roll, and I

had numerous academic accolades. Everyone boasted about my potential. My family was already broken, and I didn't want to bring a baby into our chaos, especially with no dad to support me. I finally made the heartbreaking and selfish decision to get the abortion.

Four hundred dollars was the going price. I had no job and no money, but Pierre and his parents were happy to supply the funds. The fact that his parents knew and supported the decision was mind blowing to me. It must have been normal just like everyone else had said.

I was four weeks pregnant, and the day of the abortion was a school day, which meant I had to sneak out and go. I was dropped off at school and kept a low profile. My best friend knew about my plans and was prepared to cover for me should anyone ask my whereabouts. Luckily, I had good grades and great attendance, so no one would bat an eye at my sudden absence from school. Pierre picked me up and took me to the appointment.

The forty-minute ride was quiet. Jay-Z's *Blueprint* album played as he drove. When "Song Cry" came on, something about the introduction, especially the sample of Bobby Glenn's "Sounds Like a Love Song," made me cry uncontrollably. The track was a perfect ballad that mirrored the pain in my heart as I cried. I didn't want to have the abortion, but I felt the pressure, and I really believed I didn't have another choice.

The traumatic experience began with the nurse taking me into a small room and having me sit on a table with stirrups. She gave me some medicine that was supposed to make me sleep during the procedure, but I was awake for the whole thing. There was a monitor near my head. I guess it was used to find the baby. They turned on a loud machine that sounded like a vacuum, and it suctioned the baby from my womb. I had seen the baby moving inside me on the monitor, but when the machine turned on, I saw nothing. I cried before finally passing out.

I woke up in a purple room surrounded by multiple beds, still feeling drugged, and I could barely walk. Pierre gave me an ultrasound picture of the baby the clinic had given him, which was just another dagger to my heart. I felt horrible. I was discharged and slept during the car ride back.

I was still feeling the effects of the drugs, so Pierre brought me back to his house to feed me and allow me to nap until the drugs wore off. I heard a conversation he was having with his mother upstairs as I woke up. She was confirming that we had gone through with the abortion. He said, "Yes," and she said, "Good."

I began crying and went to his bathroom in the basement, which signaled to him that I was awake. He came back downstairs with food, and I told him I was ready to go back to school.

"We're not going to talk about this?" he asked.

"No, we're not. You got what you wanted, so what do we need to discuss?"

"This was my first time having one, and I didn't know I'd feel like this, too. We can try again for another one."

I gave him a blank stare and asked to be taken back to school.

When I walked into school, I went to my scheduled English class, dropped to the floor, and laid my head on my best friend's lap, sobbing. She rubbed my head and told me it would be okay. I had to suck it up, though, as I had to participate in the senior class elections. I was running for class secretary. I'd been crying all day and looked a hot mess, yet I got on that stage with no preparation, gave my speech, and, surprisingly, I pulled it off and won.

The days following were rough. My emotions were all over the place. I had to secretly take the prescribed medication while dealing with the shame of what I had done. And now, Tyler wanted his space after we got into a fight, so my mom and I moved back in with my aunt and cousin. I had no emotions to give and didn't care. I still had a key to my dad's house, so I would go hang out at his home while he was at work to have some me time and try to forget the unforgettable.

8

Out of Control

ON SEPTEMBER 24, 2001, I was going through a lot of emotions that my mom didn't understand. Arguing was constant between us, and on this day, my frustrations with her reached an all-time high. While over my dad's house, instead of just chilling like I would do on occasion, I cleaned up the house for him. I washed dishes, cleaned the bathroom, cleaned his room, and did laundry while also pulling out his fall/winter clothes because it was getting cold. My mom called and said she was on her way. I knew how to time her, but this day, she arrived earlier than I anticipated and decided to come into the house. Usually, she'd pull up, and I'd come out, but she decided to come inside. She walked through the front door with a look of disgust. She went from room to room seeing what I had done and was pissed.

"Oh, so you came over here and cleaned up for him after all he's put me through?"

I stood there mute. I didn't have the energy to argue back with her; I couldn't care less.

"Let's go!"

The argument lasted through the night and into the next morning. She couldn't understand why I would clean up the house and help him out. My mom hated that I didn't show clear disdain for him like she did. I got my love and support from him, so I was conflicted. I knew what he'd done was wrong, but from him I got the most hugs and the most laughs, and he took care of me financially.

While I was getting ready for school, it dawned on me that I wanted to live with my dad. I couldn't take it anymore. We were stuck in a cycle of insanity and I'd had enough of it.

The ride to school made my blood boil. She would not stop yelling at me, and my anger rose more and more, further solidifying my decision to leave. Somehow, she knew I would skip school to spend time with my dad sometimes when I was mad at her. I had no clue as to how she knew. My principal knew the family situation and that I was skipping my classes, but he didn't mind because I was passing all my classes with flying colors and ranked in the top ten percent of my class.

As I got out of the car, thinking I could finally get some peace of mind, she got out as well. "You're not slick! I'm going in here to tell your principal not to let you go anywhere with your daddy!" she snapped.

I froze and stared at her as she proceeded to walk into the school. As I followed her into the office so we could both talk to him, she pushed me toward my classroom. "This is none of your business," she said.

I was beyond pissed off. This was the last straw. I'd had enough.

I had just completed level two of driver's training and had the spare keys to the car. I mentally plotted how to get her back. When my mom left my dad the last time, she had taken his new car, and he fussed every time we went to visit him. "I'm paying four hundred dollars a month for a car I don't even get to drive, and I'm driving a two-door hatchback Focus." I planned to take the car back to Daddy and let her see how it felt. I hopped in the car, and the adventure began.

My school was in a predominantly white neighborhood, so I

knew if she called the police, they'd be there in seconds. I sped to my dad's house to get the car to him. His home was only ten minutes away from the school, so I didn't see it as an impossible task. Plus, I plotted to drive another route, where the police were less likely to show up. I was crying while driving and doing ninety mph down a side street in the rain. It was a recipe for disaster. "Song Cry" by Jay-Z was on repeat. I was beginning to think it was the soundtrack to my life. The abortion, my parents, and all the fighting weighed on my heart as I sped down the side streets. I briefly paused for stop signs. The rain was pouring down. I wasn't familiar with the streets, but I knew my mom's meeting with my principal wouldn't take long, and she would be calling the police soon. I turned the music up louder and cried harder.

I was going so fast that I began to hydroplane, causing me to lose control of the car. I tried to regain control but failed. I heard a loud pop like a gunshot.

I awoke to the sight and smell of smoke and my ears ringing; the airbag had deployed from the steering wheel. I jumped out of the car because I thought it was about to explode. All I could do was scream and cry for help in the middle of the road. Blood spewed from my mouth as I screamed—a lot of blood.

An older woman came to me from a nearby house, but I kept crying and screaming, looking back at the car. As I looked back at the accident scene, I was able to determine what happened. The car had jumped the curb hitting a transformer utility pole, which split and fell. The Lord's grace was upon me because the car should have been deadlocked into the center of the pole, causing it to split and land on the car. I could've easily been electrocuted if just one of the wires from the power lines had touched the car. The older lady brought me into her house and tried to calm me down, but I kept screaming and crying for my dad. She gave me a towel to hold up to my mouth while I talked.

The woman and her family were trying to use their cell

phones to call 9-1-1. If risking my life and damaging my parents' car wasn't enough, I had caused a six-block power outage as well (and a $40,000 bill). The woman let me use a cell phone, and I called my dad, but he didn't answer. I called my grandparents, who lived a block away, but my grandmother didn't believe me.

The police and ambulance came and treated me, but when they helped me off the couch, pain surged through my body, and I screamed. I wanted to wait until my dad came, but the police and ambulance wanted to get me to the hospital immediately.

"How did you crash?" the police asked me.

"It was raining. I heard gunshots, and I panicked and lost control of the car, and next thing I remember is waking up to smoke." I purposely left out the details of my mother and the school incident.

There were no gunshots, just me hitting the pole and the sounds of the pole snapping and crashing down near the car. They put a neck brace on me because it hurt to turn my neck, but my back ached the worst. They loaded me into the ambulance and strapped me down on the board. The bumpy trip to the hospital made my body ache even more. It seemed like the ambulance hit every bump imaginable.

As I was rushed into ER, my tongue was still bleeding. I was still in pain and continued to cry. I finally saw my dad, and I cried even more, apologizing for totaling the car. He shushed me and told me not to worry, that I was more important. He rubbed my head and held my hand.

There was a wait, and they took me to get x-rays. That's when my mom showed up. As soon as she walked into the x-ray room, she gave me the dirtiest look ever. I was used to it. It was the same way she looked at me daily, but I thought, this time, she would have some empathy. Seeing her daughter lying in pain on a stretcher wearing a neck and back brace with a bloody mouth didn't faze her one bit. Seconds after the look of death, she and my dad began arguing.

"This is all your fault!" she yelled at him.

"My fault? You're the one who left. This is your fault!" he clapped back.

"Well, why did I leave, huh? Ask yourself that question!"

I couldn't believe this was happening. I was enraged. I began wailing, and a doctor came in, which made them both stop. After the x-rays, I went back to my assigned room, and my mother and dad glared at each other.

I was finally discharged and given a bunch of pain meds. I left with a knot on my head from when the woodgrain steering wheel had hit me on impact. The doctor told me I would have to go to physical therapy because I'd have permanent back pain due to a herniated disc and I'd bit my tongue almost in two from the impact, so I needed stiches.

When I was discharged and we were walking out, I thought World War III was about to break out. My grandmother and mother exchanged dirty looks. My granddad was happy to see me, but Mallory was not. Mallory had brought my mom, so we had to leave with her. As soon as I got into the car, she showed no mercy and immediately began cussing me out.

"I don't care what happened! You shouldn't be skipping school. See, you got Daddy fooled. I know you were being stupid trying to go see some boy. Now, look what you've caused! Now Mama ain't got no car. A $50,000 car is totaled because you wanted to skip and go to your boyfriend. I know what you were doing. You need your butt beat!"

I sat silently in the backseat, still crying. I wasn't skipping school, but no one wanted to hear that. We rode past the accident scene because my mom said she wanted to take pictures to show me how I could've lost my life, and she didn't want me to forget. The accident scene was blocked off because the electric company was trying to rectify the power outage.

The junkyard where the car was located was up the street. My mom told the junkyard owners that it was ours, and I was the one who had caused the accident. The owners were dumbfounded. They were convinced that no one had survived but concluded that the airbag must have saved my life. They explained that there's an airbag above the seatbelt in luxury cars, and when the car swerved out onto the street, my head should have swung left out of the window, but the airbag had deployed and threw my head back opposite the window.

We went into the back of the junkyard to look at the car, and it was, indeed, totaled. The front bumper was detached and sitting on the hood of the car. All the tires were blown out and the wheels were still cocked to the right. I was numb as my mom took pictures. When she finished, we left and went back to my aunt's house.

Getting over the accident was rough, especially since my abortion had been just a week prior. My body hadn't yet recovered, and now I had to also heal from a car accident. I missed school for about two weeks but had company every day. The students at school made me a big card, but they also spread various rumors about how I'd tried to kill myself. I was beyond irritated.

Pierre found out about my accident and came over while Mallory was at the house with me.

As we sat on the couch, I saw his car pull up through the living room blinds. Until then, none of my family had seen him. I was hoping he'd send a text to get my approval to come to the door, but he didn't.

As he got out of the car and approached the door, Mallory jumped up from the couch in a fit of anger. "Why is Pierre here at this house?"

Clueless as to how Mallory recognized him, I shrugged. The situation happened too quickly for me to come up with an excuse off the top of my head, and I really didn't know why he was there. We were over, and I didn't know how he was made aware of my accident.

Mallory opened the door. "Yes?"

"I came to see Tiffany and see how she's doing."

"You are not welcome at this house to see her, and don't ever come back over here."

Mallory watched him pull out of the driveway before slamming the door closed. "What the hell is wrong with you? Is this the guy you've been sneaking around with?"

I refused to answer. I knew anything I would say would be used against me.

My mom quickly interjected. "Mallory, what is the problem? Who was that?"

"Who *was* that? He's one of the most dangerous hoodlums in the city. Plus, he's twenty-five!"

"Tiffany!" my mom screeched.

"I didn't know," I said and began crying instantly.

I wouldn't have classified him as a hoodlum because I saw a softer side of him. I did know he carried guns; I just never knew the reason. After we added sex to the relationship, I began going over his house more frequently. Upon my arrival, he'd pull his gun out from around the back of his waistline and place it under the couch cushion. I never thought anything about it. I actually felt safer seeing it.

I felt for him far beyond my first two boyfriends, but there was no way I could stay with him after he'd made me have an abortion. But my heart smiled knowing he cared enough to show his face and check on me. I didn't know if he ever tried contacting me again after Mallory dismissed him from the house. My mom was furious and immediately took my phone. She had no words for how disappointed she was; all I knew was I was on lock down.

Eventually, I bounced back and, about a month later, my parents got back together. Many claimed I'd caused the accident to make them reconcile, but that wasn't the case. My anger had gotten the best of me, and I made a horrible decision that almost took my life. I had a newfound independence, dating and hanging out with friends, but now, because of my dumb mistakes, my parents were reunited, and all my fun was about to come to an abrupt halt. My mother claimed she got back with my dad because she felt their split was affecting me for the worse, and I was out of control, from dating "hoodlums," to skipping school, and stealing cars. However, their back and forth shenanigans made me numb. I added "This Can't Be Life" by Jay-Z to my soundtrack.

My dad still worked afternoons, and we were back home— again. Thankfully, my mom still allowed me to have a social life and my dad agreed to allow me to hang with a few of my trusted friends. My cousin Danielle and I stopped fighting as we got older and started hanging out together over the weekends.

There was a guy in my class who was a mocha cutie. He made me laugh with his humor. He was genuine and had a good family upbringing. In December 2001, we began dating. It felt authentic, and we quickly became a couple. This was my first real relationship. I hadn't seen the other guys much. They didn't go to my school, and they did their own thing with other girls. He was the star basketball player, and he had a lot of female fans. I quickly noticed that I possessed the same jealousy my dad had. Hearing other girls cheering for him resulted in me giving grim looks and bullying them. I didn't like him talking to other girls and would instantly catch attitudes with him and accuse him of cheating. Depending on who the girls were and how extra they were being with him, I would even go as far as threatening them. I was the aggressor, and when I didn't get what I wanted, I made sure to manipulate and control him with my tears to get my way.

I made it my business to be around him all day at school and after school when I could. I did everything in my power to keep an eye on him. I would backdoor him, too, by asking his friends about things he was doing when he wasn't in my sight. I played detective, trying to find out who was around him. I liked him so much that I started to justify why my dad acted the way he did. I began to think to myself, *Oh, when you like someone a lot, you have to control them. You keep them in close range and on a short leash. You control what they do and who they see, right?* Nah, maybe not, but, hey, no one ever talked to me about relationships. I was only going off what I'd witnessed.

I loved his family, too, so I made a conscious effort to show them that my parents had raised me well. I gave his parents the illusion that I was brought up with little to no dysfunction. After all, I wanted to marry their son, mainly because my parents were married during my dad's senior year of high school (my mom's junior year), so it wasn't like it was impossible.

Home life seemed to have a little normalcy until February 2002, when the fighting and arguments between my parents began again. Dion had listed my mom as the contact person for the church daycare that cared for his daughter. The church called for my mom, and when the number showed on the caller ID, my dad accused her of dating the pastor. He yanked her by her arm, demanding an explanation before going to work. My mom told him he was going to regret putting his hands on her. After more arguing, he finally went to work.

Mom picked me up from school. As I got into the car, she didn't greet me and was stone faced with her sunglasses on. I instantly knew something wasn't right.

"What's wrong?" I asked.

"Your daddy put his hands on me again, and I've had enough. I'm going to kill him, or he's going to kill me. Enough is enough. I'm divorcing him. I've had the locks changed, and I filed a PPO."

I was speechless and fearful. I needed to get home to call my boyfriend and share with him because I was secretly terrified. I was happy she was ending it, but I didn't know how my dad was going to take this or what he would do.

I sat on the phone with my boyfriend, looking out my bedroom window that faced the front of our house, and like clockwork, my dad pulled into the driveway at eleven p.m. from work. He tried unlocking the door with his keys and failure greeted him.

He knocked on the door, only to be met by my mom's response: "I told you don't come back. I told you that was the last time you put your hands on me!"

"Open this motherfuc**** door right now!" The knocks turned into banging.

My boyfriend could hear the commotion and told me to hang up with him and call the police ASAP. I followed his instructions, and the police came quickly. I could hear the sirens in the distance, and when my dad heard them, he backed out of the driveway, speeding. The police came and took pictures of the bruise on my mom's arm and the damage to the doors. After all the years of abuse, the police had finally made their way inside the house to document the damage. My mom had found her voice; she wasn't afraid anymore. This time, she was going to stay faithful to her word and wasn't going to turn back.

Sadly, I had become so numb to their merry-go-round over the years that none of it fazed me.

I was dangerously in love with my high school sweetheart. After my mom put my dad out, she was overly emotional about their split, which caused her to act out toward me. I avoided being home as much as I could. I shared with my boyfriend's parents what was happening at home so I could spend more time with him, and they were okay with it. I initiated adding sex to our relationship. I'd gone too long without my drug, and now that the pressures were up again with my family drama, I needed a release.

The great thing about my boyfriend was that sex wasn't my only outlet with him. He was my new outlet in general. My mom became even angrier during the divorce process. He was my way of escaping all her drama, the mood swings and all. We were inseparable, together all day at school, in the same classes, after school at his basketball games and practices, then at his house. On the weekends, we did activities with his family. I avoided my home as much as possible. My school performance didn't drop. I still maintained good grades, straight A's, except a C in calculus. I was accepted into five colleges and was ready to live it up.

Mallory and I were the only ones to experience prom. Tyler forked over a lot of money for me to go, and I appreciated him for it. He paid for everything, from my hair, to my nails, and the dress. I didn't have a clue about all the sacrifices he'd made for me just to ensure my senior year was taken care of. My mother went out of town with her friends to a church convention and wasn't there to see me off or take any pictures with me in my dress. I didn't understand or agree with her choice, and I was furious about it. But I shrugged it off and left it bottled up inside. I had to act like a big girl as usual because life's disappointments were my normal. Tyler was there, though, co-parenting as usual, and even Mallory came with her friends, so I enjoyed the pre-prom activities.

Prom itself sucked, as my high school sweetie broke the news that he was moving to another state for college, which wasn't in the plan for our future. His breaking news started an argument between us. My expectation for prom night was for it to be full and long lasting, going into the early hours of the next day. Instead, I was home by midnight.

My high school graduation was horrible. My parents had been arguing throughout the divorce process, and with the restraining order still active against my dad, he refused to come. Even if he wanted to rebel against the PPO and risk it all to be with me, my mom would've called the cops on him to block him from being around her. My grandparents also refused to come and share the moment with me because they supported their son. I was part of the collateral damage.

Anger encompassed me, and I blamed by mom. I was heartbroken. I was the last child to graduate, and my dad should've seen it along with my grandparents. I had earned and deserved that moment. I felt my parents owed me a truce for one day, especially with all the hell I had endured over the years and all the drama they had stirred up during my senior year. I was so livid that I didn't want to be around my family. I made plans to celebrate with my boyfriend and his family. However, my escape plan with my boyfriend didn't last long. We broke up a week after graduation. That's when everything started hitting me, and I was forced to see the reality of my circumstances.

9

Me, Myself, and I

WITH THE DIVORCE DISMANTLING our immediate family, my mother began gravitating more toward her family, which was understandable. However, I didn't want them forced on me. Every experience I had with them had been unpleasant. I wanted nothing to do with them, but my mom needed them during this time in her life, I guess. And just like I thought, sooner than later, they struck again.

I'd been fighting since my parents first separated when I was nine. I had to fight to be seen, to be heard and understood. I had to fight to defend myself and clarify misinterpretations that were thrown my way. I became a fighter. The fighter in me birthed and fueled the competitor in me. It drove my hunger to be better than everyone because I was sick and tired of being labeled as something I wasn't, being undervalued and overlooked.

Danielle was two weeks older than me, and although we weren't physically fighting, because of our past, I still wanted to beat her. She became my competition. I was already on the school grind, but since she was back in my life, I was determined to continue to show her up in academia. I wanted to shine and leave her in the shadows. I also wanted to be accepted by my mom's family because they had severely misinterpreted me.

I thought my grades would make me stand out. Good grades were rewarded and celebrated on my dad's side. However, my cousin received a block party to celebrate her graduation with family who had traveled in from out of town, but I received nothing. I was furious, and the fact that my mother wanted me to attend the party was even more absurd to me. Here I was accepted into the top colleges, graduating at the top of my class with numerous awards, and I didn't even get a congratulations from them, but Danielle could get a full-blown party; I was heartbroken.

Mom was so consumed with the divorce proceedings that she didn't notice I was catching the brunt of it. I hit a breaking point and moved out in July 2002. I was working two jobs and supporting myself anyway, and there were only two months left before going away to college. I moved in with a family friend, determined to show my mother I could make it on my own without her.

Tyler and Lindsay, a family friend, took turns lending me their cars, so there was no need to go home because of transportation issues. My grind was working out well, and I was excelling at my new jobs. It was critical for me to provide for myself and not fall into the trap of having to go back with my mom. Part of me learned that from Mallory's example. She'd been the role model on how to take care of business since she was sixteen, when she'd landed her first job and multiple jobs thereafter, and I followed in her footsteps.

August 24, 2002 was move-in day for college. Tyler and I got to campus bright and early for registration and move in. My roommates had already arrived and we met. But I had to go back home. My dad bought me a mini-refrigerator, and I needed to go pick it up. I told my new roommates I had to make a quick run to grab the fridge, but I'd meet them later for the festivities. I called my mom to tell her I was coming to grab it from the house, and I could tell by her lack of response that she wasn't pleased. I get it—just a few weeks prior marked the conclusion of their nasty divorce, and it was finally official. Their marriage was finished. To make matters worse, the courts had sided with my dad, as he'd manipulated the judge, and they treated my mom like she didn't deserve to have anything. My dad came to court wearing his preacher collar, stating his case of being a good, law-abiding citizen and preacher. He explained that my mom had stolen from him each time she left. He even threw in there how my mom had damaged his knees, knowing she was defending herself. And after thirty years of marriage, my mom barely got anything from the divorce. She felt like she was reliving the abuse through the court system. So when my dad started dropping off gifts like he was the perfect parent, it upset her.

My dad left the mini fridge in the backyard to avoid being around my mother. When Tyler and I showed up, we didn't notice it immediately. We went into the house. "Hey, Ma. Daddy left me a fridge for school. Where is it?" I asked.

Tyler had already found it in the backyard and was putting it into his car. I didn't get the memo yet and was met by an aggressively angry mother.

"Oh, so all the hell I go through, and you just gonna take gifts from him?"

"Ma, it's college move-in day, and I needed a fridge," I explained.

She slammed me into the backdoor. "What about what I need? All the hell I've been through, everything I've lost, and you side with him!" she yelled.

I understood her pain, but going off on a tangent and roughhousing me wasn't necessary. I had done nothing wrong. I didn't want to be bruised up on my move-in day, so I grabbed her wrists. "Ma, *stop*! I'm not taking sides! I just need a fridge for college. Chill!" I pushed her back and ran toward the car.

Tyler was already waiting in the running car. I jumped in and yelled, "Go, go, go, go, and don't stop!"

We ran the corner stop sign, but we were forced to wait at the next one that led into major traffic. We burned rubber while turning when we finally could, and I told Tyler what was happening. When I looked back, my mom was about a quarter mile away from us; she had just turned from that same corner, chasing us at a high speed. I called our dad in a panic.

"Daddy, I went to get the fridge, and Mama flipped on me and tried jumping on me. I grabbed her wrists and pushed her back and ran. Now she's chasing us."

Earlier, my dad had told me to stop at my grandparents' house after picking up the fridge before going back to campus, so we were on our way there, but he told us to change direction. "Oh no, I'm so sorry," he said. "Get on I-94 east and go to Detroit. Keep driving, and I'll tell you where to get off once you cross over the Michigan Ave. exit." My dad told me to call him back.

"Okay," Tyler said. He kicked the speed into high gear, breezing through yellow lights like we were in the Daytona 500. We lost my mom as we hopped onto the freeway. I called my dad back and let him know we'd passed the exit he'd referenced and he told us where to meet him. We met him down the street from the Wayne State University restaurant. He greeted me with a hug, one of those hugs that felt like they had magic powers. A hug that would morph me back into Baby Tiff, where the world was about strawberry shortcake ice cream, McDonald's Happy Meals, and strawberry shakes. A hug that made me feel most loved. His hug made me break down and cry after I'd been doing such a good job of internalizing the pain. It sucked to see the state my parents were in, where our family was. Not to mention, it was college move-in day.

Needless to say, move-in day sucked. By the time I got back to campus at around eleven p.m., I had missed everything because of the drama. This was what my life was reduced to. Whenever something significant came up, my parents' drama destroyed it.

I wasn't excited about living with three other girls. As the baby of the family, I never had to share much, especially not a room. My roommates were all about that college life, wanting to experience everything it had to offer. I, on the other hand, was about chasing money. They went to all the parties and were excited about campus activities while I just needed a few hours of sleep. I had a full-time class load, fifteen credit hours, while working two jobs. My three roommates were constantly screaming at the top of their lungs, laughing, singing, and doing girlie stuff. And one of them was on the phone with her boyfriend *all the time*, especially late at night. I hated it because I wasn't a girlie girl, and I'd never had those slumber party experiences to connect with other girls. I was like Oscar the Grouch. I just wanted to be alone and in peace.

I began developing a passive-aggressive personality. I didn't know how to communicate my needs, wants, and requests, so I decided to teach indirect lessons without confrontation. I shut them out and didn't talk, played music loudly to drown out their conversations, and isolated myself from them and their activities.

I didn't do the boyfriend thing coming into college. I had just broken up with my high school sweetie, so listening to my roommates drove me crazy because they all had boyfriends, and I was a lone wolf. I didn't like to share, either. Just because we were in a common space didn't mean my stuff belonged to them. My dad had raised us on the principle, "God bless the child who has their own," and I'd adopted that as my mantra. I'd had enough taken from me in my lifetime already. I was not sharing. My roommates liked to use things that were in the common space, and I wasn't for it. Taking my stuff without my permission was a trigger for my anger. Although they were trivial things like my snacks, pencils, and notepads, I felt what was theirs was theirs and what was mine was mine.

My roommates sometimes lived like we were in a bachelorette pad, which led me to be passive aggressive by slamming things when I cleaned instead of just communicating that I was upset about the dirty room. I wanted out fast, but there was nothing I could do until next semester.

I was focused and headstrong about getting money and hitting the books. I desperately needed to learn balance. I was taking fifteen college credits my first semester while working part-time on campus then heading to the mall where I worked in the evenings. Then I came in from work to study late at night and do my homework. I was tired.

I soon learned that some of Mallory's friends were attending the same college. They took me under their wings and let me hang out with them. They also checked on me frequently. I thought I was large and in charge. You couldn't tell me nothing. Known as Ebony and Ivory Productions, they threw parties on campus and asked me if I wanted to work the door to get some of the profit. That became my third job. The parties were on Thursday nights, sometimes Fridays. It took a toll on me quickly because I had early Friday classes, and I barely made it due to being so tired from working the door for the party the night before. But I was getting money, so I felt I was doing something right. I was always taught by Mallory and my dad how to grind but never how to rest. But if you don't make time for rest, rest will force you to make time. I was headed for burnout quick, fast, and in a hurry. I decided I needed to decrease my class load, so I let go of the mall job.

My roommate, Tori, was also friends with my cousin, Danielle, whom I'd grown to love. We met from hanging out together during senior year, and she was hilariously funny and chill like I was, so we decided to become roomies. She was always inviting me somewhere, and I always turned her down until one Friday night.

"Tiff, Tiff," Tori said.

"What up, T?"

"You're all work and no fun, and that makes you quite boring."

"What you got up today, T?"

"Well, your cousin and I are going down to Henry's Palace in the D. You down?"

"What is a Henry's Palace?" I asked.

"It's a male strip club, but it's not like a for real strip club. They dance more like Dru Hill, Jagged Edge type routines."

"Well, guess what, I'm going to come and take you up on your offer!"

"Awww shoot! Let's get it."

I realized I needed to have some fun. The strip club was well known, and Tori was right, it wasn't the traditional strip club because the dancers were fully clothed and had dance battles with New Edition routines. I wasn't as turned off as I thought I would be.

"Let me go get my drinks," Danielle said.

Drinks? I thought. She must've meant Pepsi or Coke or something.

She came back with a drink that contained plenty of alcohol.

"How'd you get that? We aren't twenty-one," I said.

"That's why we come here. Notice we're here early, too. They allow underage drinking. They don't card at the bar when you get here early," she said.

Sure enough, the dancers came out and started battle dancing. It was pretty hype. I took a sip of Danielle's drink, and that was enough for me. I never drank much, just a few sips and I was done. Mallory played a huge part in my drinking habits. She taught me a hard lesson early on about knowing my limit.

One time, when I decided I wanted to drink and smoke with Mallory, she said, "Oh, so you think you bad?"

"I can hang," I said confidently.

She smirked and nodded. "Okay."

She gave me the blunt. "Smoke this," she said and followed by giving me a cup of Hennessey straight. "Drink this."

We continued until I said I'd had enough and fell asleep on the floor. I woke up slightly and felt my head spinning. I was nauseated and quickly stood and ran to the bathroom. I threw up immediately. I felt like I was puking my insides out. My sister came into the bathroom during a brief puke pause and grabbed me by the hair.

"Praying to the porcelain gods, huh? Know your limit! You ain't grown. Any guy can take advantage of you by getting you pissy drunk. This is what you get."

As she released my head, more vomit flowed. Mallory dropped me off at my dorm, and I had a hangover for two days. I couldn't eat, and my head was still pounding. I was miserable. After that horrible experience, I was done with getting hammered for the sake of getting hammered.

Once the dance battles ended, the music and lights were lowered, and the dancers stripped down to their G-strings. However, Danielle was only there for the drinks, and she let them continue to flow. I didn't want her drinking and driving because that was how our granddad was killed, so I became the self-appointed designated driver.

After one month of being in college and no communication from my mom, she called me. I was surprised to see her number show up on my cell phone.

"Hello?" I said.

"What is this I'm hearing about you being out of control?" she said.

"What are you talking about?"

"I got a call from your aunt saying you've been going to strip clubs, and you're out of control!"

Danielle was the one who had initiated our strip club excursions, yet she told my mother's side of the family that I was addicted. One of my aunts called my mom to tell the details and declared I would do nothing but get pregnant and have babies. I shouldn't have paid it attention, but I did, and I was angered. It seemed my mom's side of the family was always looking for the worst in me.

"You don't even call me. You haven't called me since I've been in college to see how I'm doing or how college is going. You didn't even defend me as usual, but you're calling to take sides with your family and blame me. Have a good day, Mother."

As I hung up. The wedge between my mom and I grew even deeper. From that moment on, I was determined to prove everyone wrong.

10

Our Family Portrait

MARY J. BLIGE'S 1994 hit single, "My Life" had been the anthem of my existence thus far. Ironically, from the time I began college during my parents' divorce through all the foolishness during my freshman year of college, I masked my tears with dedication and ego. I viewed tears as a sign of weakness, and I couldn't afford to be weak. Internalization was my strength—so I thought. I bottled my feelings until I reached a breaking point. Once the tears broke free, I began to cry a lot, mostly about our family, and I slept a lot.

The lyrics to P!nk's song "Family Portrait" would leave me a sobbing mess as I listened to her sing about a family taking a picture to appear happy. My family hadn't taken a professional picture since I was younger, and after hearing the song, that was what I wanted, for us to be happy again as a unit. But that wasn't our reality. We'd become dysfunctional and broken, and a family picture wasn't going to fix it.

In early November 2002, I was at my dorm across the hall in a friends' room, dancing with them to Justin Timberlake's song "Senorita," when my roommate came and told me my cell phone was constantly ringing.

"Let me go check and see what's up. I'll be back," I told my friends.

I skipped back to my room away from the music to see multiple missed calls from my mom—something wasn't right.

I called her back. "Hey, what's up, Ma?"

My mom was crying hysterically and yelling. She was incoherent as I tried to calm her down.

"Ma, stop, breathe. Slow down. I can't understand you."

I heard her exhaling, and through her tears, she was finally calm enough to speak. "Your dad is dating Sarah!"

My eyes widened and my face was frozen by confusion. I pulled the phone away to make sure I was talking to the right person because this couldn't be right. My dad couldn't be dating my mother's best friend, the only friend he had allowed her to have.

"Are you sure? How do you know?" I asked.

"I went to Sarah's house because she hadn't been answering my calls. When I got there, I saw your daddy's car in the driveway. All I could do was drive off."

I don't remember how the call with my mom ended.

"Tiff, Tiff, Tiff! What's up? You good?" my roommate asked.

I couldn't respond. I was too busy dialing Sarah's phone number.

"Hello?" she answered.

I was seething. "I'mma beat you're a** on sight! You think you gone get away with what you did with my daddy! I'm coming for you, b****!"

She hung up on me, and I called her back repeatedly.

"Tiff, calm down. Let it go. Breathe!" my roommate said, trying to calm me down.

"Y'all need to back up off me and give me space. You don't know the details," I warned.

I continued calling Sarah nonstop, but the calls were going to voicemail. My roommates had never seen this side of me, so my rage frightened them. I paced the room before sitting on the bed.

My phone rang. It was my dad calling me back. My heart froze. I didn't want to answer, but I had to.

"You watch your mouth! I didn't raise you to talk like that to your elders, and who do you think you are, calling an adult and saying the stuff you're saying? You're not grown!" he yelled.

"I am," I snapped.

"Your mother did this. *She* divorced me. *She* put me out of my house."

I was indignant. "You *beat* her for years on end!"

"I never touched her! I'm going to be with Sarah now, and there is nothing you or your siblings can say or do about it. I'm a grown man. Since you have a problem with it, I'm done with you!"

I couldn't say a word. My lips were sealed. He was done with me? I was stifled. My heart dropped. I hung up on him and immediately rushed to sit outside my dorm because I needed air. I felt dizzy, very dizzy. The dad I had adored for eighteen years, even through his madness, the man who had raised my siblings and me, who had provided and taken care of us and claimed to love us unconditionally, had just cut me off for this woman. He abandoned us. He left me. My heart was broken. I had always been Daddy's little girl no matter what. Until now, no one could come between the bond my dad and I shared.

As I sat outside that night, everything went through my head. I envisioned the first time I saw my dad hit my mom when I was seven years old. That started the chain of events that had ruined my life. One of my roommates came outside and tried to console me. She told me to pray about it because she knew I went to church, but I wasn't trying to hear it.

As quickly as she'd come to talk to me, she left.

Pray? That word seemed foreign to me because everything I believed was flipped in one night. How could I pray to God when

I didn't understand why He would let these things happen? We had been praying for years, and it seemed as though God never answered, and tonight wasn't different. The man who preached the Word to me and taught me the Bible was the same one doing everything he'd taught me and others not to do.

Hate began to fill my heart just as quickly as it had been broken. I thought I was the only sibling who knew, but Dion called to inform me he also knew and volunteered to pick me up from campus. We decided we needed to be together because my mom wasn't taking the news well at all. I packed my things and sat back outside. My roommates came and loved on me before seeing me off. As hard as my shield was, those hugs were exactly what I needed. They went back inside, and I sat on the steps alone with my thoughts as I waited for Dion to arrive.

When I was younger, I didn't realize how disingenuous my dad could be. As I got older, the pieces started to connect. I had always given him the benefit of the doubt through the years, but I couldn't anymore.

Mallory called me. "Hey, what's up? I just arrived at Mama's house. What's going on?" she asked.

"Mama called me crying because Daddy and Sarah are dating. I called and cussed Sarah out, only for Daddy to call me back and defend her and say he's done with me."

Mallory was emotionless and quiet.

I asked her, "How is Mom?"

"She's locked herself in her room and isn't answering. Don't worry, though. I got her."

"Don't worry? How? I'm coming home."

"Tiffany, you need to stay your butt at school. I'll take care of Mom."

"Okay." I hung up.

I didn't bother telling her I was still coming home. The tears of hurt and vulnerability I had shed before stopped. Now, I was angry and spilled bitter tears because my mom was hurting. It wasn't abnormal for my mom to lock herself in the bedroom. She did that whenever she was upset and after every fight she'd had with my dad. She went into a deep depression when she was hurting.

I had a flashback of a moment when I saw my mom after my dad had beaten her. We had returned home from leaving him. I was vacuuming the living room floor and had just finished when she walked out of the bedroom and into the bathroom. She sat on the edge of the tub and started running bath water. As I walked away to put the vacuum up, I looked at her. My mom's face was swollen. Her hair was a tangled mess, and she had bruises all over her body.

I approached the side of her and offered to help her by running the bath water for her and adding Epsom salt. I rubbed her back, but she snatched away from me. "You should've helped me when I was screaming for it," she hissed.

I knew she hadn't meant to put that burden on me, but I never forgot that sight or those words. For years, I thought my failure to help her was the underlying reason our relationship was strained. I wasn't there for her in those moments; therefore, I had to do something. I couldn't just sit at my dorm, go to classes, and pretend that everything was okay while my mother endured unbearable pain at home.

I began to see my mother in a different light. For the first time, I completely sided with her and felt her pain without thinking of how my dad's feelings would be affected. I realized my mother loved my dad unconditionally. My parents had gotten married during my mom's junior year of high school, at the age of sixteen when she was pregnant with Dion. The abuse had started back then with power and control. She thought it was love because he cared for her financially, and he was a provider. That's what men did back then. She stayed because she was trying to keep the family together and protect us from being hurt and having to suffer financially. She had been abused for thirty years, and she was finally released, but she wasn't free from the love she had for the only man she'd ever known. She didn't divorce my dad because she didn't love him anymore; she divorced him because she wanted him to stop abusing her, because she wanted to live. She wanted him to change and knew he wouldn't because he'd said, many times, that he didn't have a problem. My mom feared that if she didn't end the marriage, he would kill her or she would kill him. She still loved him, and I finally realized that.

My eyes stung from crying, and I just wanted to go to sleep, but I had to apologize to my roommates before I left. They didn't deserve the way I'd shut them down, dismissed, and walked away from them. I broke down a barrier of privacy and let them in. I shared what was going on with my family. I also instructed them not to answer my dad's calls, and if they did, to tell him I wasn't there.

Dion finally arrived to pick me up and take me home. The drive home was quiet, but I could tell that Dion had been crying also.

He said one thing. "All I want to do is put my foot up in her butt."

I said, "Well, shoot, let's go over there!"

When we arrived, I banged on that woman's door for what seemed to be an hour. I threw snow at her living room windows and tore up sales papers that were left on the front porch.

She sent my dad out to handle me. "Didn't I say leave her and us alone? Get away from here now before I call the police on y'all. I ain't playing!"

My dad was threatening to call the police on us? Wow! If we hadn't gotten the point he was trying to make earlier, we now clearly saw that he was choosing her over us.

We finally drove home. When we walked into the house, Tyler and Mallory were sitting in the living room while my mom was still in her room. I decided to go into her room, and although

I was terrified to open the door, I did it. It was pitch black and silent when I spoke to her.

"Hey, Ma. I'm home."

She didn't respond. She was lying in bed, and I feared she wasn't breathing, so I touched her. She moved from one side of the bed to the other. I put my hand on my heart and let out a sigh of relief. I leaned over to her and said, "I love you" and gave her a kiss on the cheek before walking out of the grief-stricken room and proceeded to have a family meeting with my siblings.

The session consisted of Mallory, my brothers, and I fussing about how we hated our dad.

"How could he do this to Mama?" Dion said repeatedly.

Tyler was numb and oddly relaxed about the situation. "Forget him," he said. "We have to be here for Mama."

My anger and rage bubbled to the surface, causing me to remain silent. My mind was on destroy mode.

Sarah's daughter called me. "Listen b****, you better stop calling my mom. I'm way older than you, and I will stomp you and have my people on you," she said.

"I don't care how old you are; pull up! You *and* yo' people. I'm about action. You don't know me," I said.

I was even more ready to throw some punches. I didn't care how old she was or what army she had. The anger I felt would take her and them out. I was ready to fight and defend mine.

Mallory was mostly concerned about me and tried to calm me down because she knew how close our dad and I were as the baby girl. I felt betrayed. There weren't enough words to describe the love I felt for my dad. I had overlooked his faults and shortcomings through all the wrong he had done, but the first chance he got, he'd chosen someone else over me.

I went outside and sat on the chilly back porch with Mallory and broke down crying on her shoulder with an endless stream of tears. Mallory didn't say anything, and I didn't need her to. She just held me and let me cry.

In the softest voice, she said, "Daddy lost his family, and that's the biggest loss he'll face. We can make it without him. You can call me 'Daddy.'"

I laughed for the first time that night as did she. Humor was our bond and comfort food to my soul, and my soul needed the humor to stop the tears. That dreary November night was a test to either make or break us. That night marked the death of what was left of the little girl inside me. I had to transform into a woman. No more immature thinking, no more thinking about what used to be and what could be. I became cold and detached. I had shed enough tears. Why shed more? This wasn't the first time my life was flipped upside down. Sure, the man who helped create me and took care of me had just showed me he didn't care about the family or me, but how was that any different from what I'd already experienced because of him? It wasn't.

A new Tiff was rising. An angry, bitter Tiff. The Tiff who harbored hate in her heart and was going to purposely hold on to grudges. I felt justified for my emotions and the actions they birthed. My faith in people was gone. I felt abandoned. I had no trust in anything long term. If after thirty years, my parents could divorce and my dad could quickly move on to my mother's best friend and abandon his whole family, no one could be trusted.

From the age of seven to eighteen, I had been on a merry-go-round. I was forced to leave my house and live with complete strangers who made every attempt to show me I wasn't equal. They labeled me and disrespected me. No one took notice or cared to know how I felt. No one asked because no one cared. My whole life had been a struggle, and I couldn't even trust family to have my back. I didn't *have* to struggle. The adults in my life had charted a course that I never wanted to take. I was forced. I lacked the knowledge to form healthy relationships.

I felt alone.

Adjusting

Two days before Christmas Eve, a month after my mom found out about my dad's new relationship with her ex-best friend, she finally came out of her room and went out to get a job and began implementing steps for change. She started attending a church called Evangel Ministries. The founding pastor, Pastor George Bogle, had been encouraging her through his radio ministry while she kept herself isolated inside her room. If it wasn't for his ministry, I believe we would've lost my mom mentally. She had been listening to Pastor Bogle for many years, since the first time we left my dad. He had a nighttime prayer line, which she had called many times.

The first time I went there as a kid, I strongly disliked it for the same reasons I disliked the other church we had attended with Dennis and Rebecca. It was different from the Baptist world I had grown up in. I pouted during the whole service. As an adult, she could barely make me go. She went to Thursday night bible study, Sunday service, and church events, but not me. It wasn't going to happen. She wanted me back in church and, to appease her, I began going to an old church we attended when I was growing up. There was a new pastor, though, and my dad couldn't stand him, which was a win for me.

I only went to Evangel occasionally with my mom per her request. I didn't want to be a jerk to her while she was in this fragile state, but I still didn't like it. It was different from everything I'd experienced, from devotion, to worship with a praise team singing fast songs and not from a hymn book. The dress code wasn't Sunday hats and fancy dresses, and the preacher didn't wear robes. Certainly, he couldn't be a man of God without the robe. However, I had enough common sense to know this church was helping my mom heal, so I wasn't completely against it. I wanted to support her. I was still angry, but I was fulfilling my church duty of being in the building and saying I went, to check that off the list of supportive daughter duties.

It took me a while to embrace church again after everything that happened. I never stopped believing in God; I had too much fear for that, but I hadn't been going to church. I didn't understand how my dad could be a preacher, teach us the Bible from the time we got up until we went to sleep, but still made us suffer the way he had. I couldn't fathom how someone whose life was dedicated to the Word, who declared himself a bona fide Christian, could treat my mom that way. If God was so good and faithful, how did He justify this behavior and allow my parents' divorce? How could He allow no consequences for my dad for all he had done to my mom? How could other churches that profess Christ support my dad's actions and not come to my mom's defense? Why did the church folk choose to turn a blind eye to what was going on and isolate my mom? Why did we have to struggle? Was God punishing my mom for divorcing my dad? These were some of the many questions that fogged my comprehension of who God really was despite people and circumstances.

I was raised on the principle "Do as I say, not as I do." My dad applied this rule to the Bible as well. We weren't to seek understanding. We were to take the preacher by his word, and that was final. My dad was notorious for using scripture to validate his points, even if it meant using it in the wrong context. If anyone went against my dad, he bragged about how he would pray they'd get struck down. He raised us to believe that Sunday was the holy day. We weren't supposed to listen to secular music, cuss, or go to the club on that day. If we did go to the club the night before, we could at least get up and give God some time. Although I was distant from God, I held on to that tradition. Sunday was my holy day. But after six p.m., I went back to R&B. I still prayed daily before meals and tests. I always said the same prayer: Philippians 4:13, "I can do all things through Christ, who strengthens me." But after witnessing my dad's behavior, I wanted to be done with the church. I didn't feel like the traditional church girl anymore. I loved God, and nothing could change that, but I felt that church wasn't for me. I continued to go along with the traditions I'd been taught to keep my blessings, but I felt everything about church was fake. If the preacher, who could abuse his wife on Saturday night, get up on Sunday and act like he was perfect while those who knew the truth disregarded it, how could church life be the model to follow? It no longer felt genuine to me.

We as a family were adjusting yet again to our new normal. Due to overworking myself, I was missing classes because I was exhausted. Then when the family crisis hit, I ran back and forth between home and school, making sure Mom was good. I ended up on academic probation after the first semester, and though I already quit my mall job, I also stopped working the parties and focused on my on-campus jobs and my studies. Making it in college was my success ticket to prove everyone wrong, so I entered the second semester with a renewed focus to bring my grades back up. I was also trying to adjust to my new identity as my mom's rescuer, trying to provide encouragement and be her right hand for everything. I still needed balance and a way to escape from all of that, so I decided I wanted to take spring/

summer classes to improve my grades, plus stay on campus as my getaway.

It seemed as soon as I made the decision to focus, distraction was looming around the corner. I reconnected with Diondre, a friend with whom I'd lost contact. He had moved to Indiana but called me because he missed me and wanted us to explore a new relationship. He wanted me to visit him out of state. I needed a break, and it would help me escape reality, so I agreed.

We began talking and started partying. He came up to my campus for random visits while in town, but drinking and smoking was a new addition from when we'd hung out a few years back. I wasn't a heavy smoker or drinker, but he was. I played along, drinking lightly and smoking. No matter how I tried to fit in, drinking and smoking and I didn't mix. The after effects made me feel like I was spinning and would never stop.

A couple of months passed since we re-connected. It numbed my problems, but we didn't share the same feelings. We weren't exclusive; it felt more like a booty call after a great time out. I found myself traveling down a dark path with him.

I had a job on campus and worked with a super cool girl named Robin. She was a tomboy just like me and played basketball. She was six years older than me, well into her mid-twenties. I confided in her as a friend because she had a lot of job experience and had my back at work and taught me the ropes. She was the one who suggested I take spring/summer classes to help boost my grades. Occasionally, she stopped by my dorm room because it was the building across from where we worked, and we'd walk to work.

It was the last week of the fall/winter semester. Finals had ended, and I was packing up my room to prepare to move into my new space on "the Hill," the college sophomore hotspot suggested by Robin. I was excited. Diondre did a pop-up visit to see me on campus. Everyone was moving out or prepping for the Hill move, so doors were wide open, music was flowing, and laughter was in the air.

I heard a knock and came around the corner to see his face.

"Heeeeeeeey!" he said. He looked around the room and asked, "This is where you stay?"

"Yeah, for the last couple of days. Actually, moving to another part of campus. What's up, though? I didn't expect to see you."

"On my way to the city and was hungry. Wanna eat?"

As I observed his body language and, most notably, his eyes, I could tell he was high. I was irritated but obliged.

"Sure. We can go to our campus eatery. It's a short walk from here."

As we walked to the eatery, we engaged in conversation. "How's your week been?" I asked.

"Straight."

"How long are you going to be in the city?"

My answer was met with a shrug.

"Look, if you're only going to give one-answer responses and not talk, I can go back to my room and pack."

"Shut the hell up, Tiffany! You're going to pay for my food and shut up so I can leave."

Midway to the eatery, I paused in my tracks with a full-on attitude. "Who you talking to like you stupid?" I said.

"You, bit**!" he spat with a maniacal laugh.

I flipped him the middle finger and began walking back to my dorm. Robin happened to pass us on her way to our office building. "What up, Tiff? You good?" she asked.

"Yeah, I'm good."

Robin kept walking, and Diondre came running back to me, laughing. "Aye Tiff, you gotta chill the f*** out! Nah, you can't leave now!"

He grabbed me by my arm, and I tripped and fell. Instead of helping me up, he tried to drag me across the street to the eatery because the only way he could get food was with my campus card. I'd watched too many fights between my parents to allow him to treat me that way. I kicked uncontrollably and yanked my arms loose until I was able to pull away. "Let me the f*** go!" I yelled, causing a scene.

He ran toward his car, and I chased him. Flashbacks of my mother being dragged and beaten flooded my mind and enraged my soul. I wanted his head. All the commotion got Robin's attention, and she turned around to see what was happening. I ran full steam ahead with a fiery rage, giving me the power to fight him.

Robin quickly pivoted from the direction she was walking and ran toward me, intercepting by grabbing me and making me walk with her in the opposite direction, so I wouldn't get into trouble with campus police. Robin's interference allowed him enough time to get into his car and speed off. I was livid. She took me back to my dorm room via a detour and told me to calm down and focus on the move.

Per her advice, I refocused and was now living in a one-bedroom dorm with no roommate and a shared bathroom.

Shortly after the move, Diondre apologized and suggested I come back to his home for a visit to make it better. I agreed, but it was not better. The visit was all about having sex, smoking weed, and drinking. My gut didn't feel comfortable, but I tried to comfort the knots in my stomach with drinks, hoping, with every hit of the blunt, the voices in my head would quiet down.

But those internal nudges were only snoozed for so long until the alarm went off again. While sitting at the computer making a CD playlist, an email alert come through for him, and I took it upon myself to read it. It was from another girl asking when she was coming over to hang with him and his cousin again. We weren't exclusive, but I felt if we were having sex, that was something and gave me the right to have an opinion.

"Umm ... What's up with this email from Dana asking when she can come over again? Am I not the only one?"

"B****, you don't have the right to ask me nothing. Get the f*** out of my stuff." He pulled me up from the chair.

Here he was putting his hands on me again, but this time, there was no space and no Robin to pull me away. We got into a wrestling match. My mind replayed my mom and dad's fights in my head, escalating my anger from ten to 200. I grabbed his face while he pulled my hair to make me stop until his friend pulled us apart.

That was it, my last straw. I had to leave.

"Take me back to my dorm," I demanded.

"I ain't taking you nowhere. Figure it out!"

I couldn't stay there a minute longer. Those internal nudges were blaring fire alarms warning against the forthcoming issues. I had to think quickly about who I was going to call to get me from Indiana.

There was only one person I knew would drop what she was doing and come to me. I had to bite the bullet and call my mom. I lied about what occurred and made her believe I needed to get back to school for an important assignment that I had to complete. She didn't fight me on it and came immediately. I took my bag and waited outside.

The wait felt like eight hours and had me all in my feelings and in deep reflection. I felt like I was internally dying the few short months Diondre and I had been connected. I knew this wasn't what love should be about. I couldn't grasp how I ended up in this space. After everything I'd seen, how had I now become involved in an abusive relationship? There was no way I would repeat my mom's cycle, and there was absolutely no way I could tell anyone in my family. Everyone was going through their own stuff.

My mom showed up, and she was on the phone, so thankfully,

we didn't have to have a conversation on the way back into town and to my dorm.

My dorm was my haven. Spring/summer classes were kicking off the following week, so I had a couple of days to recover from the previous day's events. Some of my friends who lived across from my old room in the old dorm moved into the same building one floor up, so I made myself come out of my shell and engage with campus culture and have fun with them. We walked to classes a lot, went to off-campus eats, and had late-night hall shenanigans and karaoke nights. I was slowly allowing myself to enjoy college life a little. My mom was doing a lot better with church and picked up a part-time job, and she seemed to be in a much better place, so I didn't need to go home as much, which allowed me to gain a lot of ground with working on my grades. Robin taught me better study skills that I used to become increasingly focused. She had a late start to college but was also driven to get her degree. I enjoyed learning and having a study buddy. I quickly implemented her study skills, which put a bump in my GPA going into the next fall/winter semester.

One afternoon, while taking a midday nap after class, I became really hot. I woke up to find my fan was off. There was no power on the alarm clock, and I was unable to use my cell phone. *What's happening?* I thought. I looked out my window to see everyone in the dorms hanging out in the middle of the courtyard. My homegirl knocked on my door.

"Hey, what's up? The power out?" I asked.

"Yeah, girl, so everybody about to party."

"Oh, okay. Well, I'm going to see if I can get a ride home."

I packed up a bookbag and went to the courtyard and found one of my homeboys, Julian. I offered him twenty dollars, and he took me home.

Upon pulling up to the driveway, I saw my dad's car. *What's going on with this here?* I thought. We had exiled him, excommunicado. Why was he there?

"Thanks, Julian," I said as I jumped out of his truck quickly.

I walked up the driveway to go in through the back door, and my dad appeared and greeted me in the kitchen.

"Hey, Tiff! What you doing home?"

Sir, what are you doing at my home is the question, I thought. My expressionless face was greeting enough for him to know it wasn't like the old days when Little Tiff jumped into his arms for hugs and smiles. I hadn't seen nor talked to my dad since November 2002, and here it was August 2003.

My mom appeared from around the corner, mirroring his greeting with an accompanying hug. She almost never hugged me. Something was off.

She saw the confusion on my face and said, "Well, I wasn't expecting you home."

"Clearly," I said as I set my bookbag down, not taking my eyes off my dad. "The power is out at school, and I can't use my cell phone either."

Within a matter of minutes, Mallory and Tyler showed up through the back door, too.

"What up, what up?" said Mallory.

As they entered the kitchen, my dad greeted them as well. Their reactions and greetings echoed mine. My mom was taken aback as to why everyone was home.

"What is everybody doing here?" she asked.

"Well, there's a national blackout," said Tyler.

At that moment, they noticed that the power was out in the house, too.

"Let me go check on my parents and see if I can get the generator running for them," my dad said as he rushed out.

We looked at our mom with judgement written all over our faces.

"What?" she asked.

Mallory was the most outspoken of us all, so she led the way.

"You know what! Why is he here? Y'all getting back together? Never mind that you know he's with your best friend!"

"I had him first, and I can take him back if I want," Mom argued.

Tyler, Mallory, and I looked at each other with expressions that said, "You have to be kidding me." I wanted to puke, but she seemed happy. Could it be that my childhood hope and dream of my parents reconciling was coming true? Just as quickly as the thought came, the next one took over, reminding me how he had chosen that new woman over us and had no communication with us. I didn't want it to be true, but as long as my mother was happy, I had nothing to say.

Our dad returned from checking on our grandparents, but we didn't have it in us to fake like we were a happy family with him, so my siblings and I decided to drive to Dion's house and have a game night. It was the first time we collectively did anything fun since our parents' divorce. Things seemed to be trending up. My grades were on the come up, we were bonding as a family, and I was feeling pretty good.

A week into my sophomore year, Diondre popped up once more for a surprise visit to campus. My old roommates were still staying together in my old dorm and didn't know what had occurred between us during the summer, so they gave him my new location. After a series of knocks, I went to the door to see who it was, but the peephole was blacked out. I thought it was one of my friends playing around, so I opened the door.

"What up!" he said.

Shocked it was him, my hyped spirit quickly turned to distress. My stomach instantly churned into knots because I was not feeling him, and I was irritated that he was there. How did he even know I was there? He walked in, and I closed the door, not locking it because I hoped this would be a short visit. He, however, was excited to see me.

"What's up, Tiff? This room is different from the last one.

More privacy, huh?" He looked around with admiration in his eyes. I didn't respond and quickly sat on my bed with my arms crossed. My dorm room was the size of a shoe box with no space for a couch. As he paced the room's aisleway in awe, I could tell by his body language that he was high again.

He wanted me to be equally excited, but I wasn't.

"Why you acting like that? You should be excited to see me," he said.

"Nah, I'm not. What's up? What are you doing here?"

He sat on the bed next to me. "You ain't miss me?" He leaned in to kiss me.

I moved back. "Nah, I didn't, and I'm not having sex with you." I pushed him off to let him know it wasn't going down like that.

"You know you want some. Come on." He tried to lean back in for a kiss.

"I said no." I pulled away and grabbed my phone through the gap in my bed frame to call Robin, who stayed in the neighboring building. She carried blades and had a gun, so I needed her to come over to show him this wasn't a game. The phone only rang twice before he got off the bed to hang it up and snatch the cord out of the wall. He returned to me and forcefully grabbed my legs, pulling my pants down as I yelled for him to stop.

He overpowered me and lay on top of me so I couldn't punch him while he tried to pull down his hoop shorts. I wiggled to make it difficult for him. When he finally got his shorts and underwear down, I heard the door shut as Robin walked into my room, her eyes wide as she took in the scene in front of her. She immediately yanked him off me and pulled her blade out, pointing it at him as he pulled his pants up.

"Yo! You can't be coming in somebody room that ain't yours," he said.

"You shouldn't be trying take sex from someone who don't want it," she retorted.

"Man, she wanted it. You don't even know."

I hurried to pull my pants up, visibly shaken.

"Get the f*** out, now!" Robin yelled.

He laughed. "It wasn't that serious. This is what we do. Tiff, tell her."

I couldn't speak. I was sitting on the edge of the bed in tears because my insides were shaking.

"Tiff, Tiff! Why the f*** aren't you putting her in her place? Man, f*** you! You, too, dyke b****!" he said as he walked out.

Robin followed him out of my room, never once backing down and keeping the blade pointed at his chest. When he was gone, she came back in and locked the door. I was still in shock. Robin hugged me, and all I could do was cry uncontrollably.

"It's cool. I got you," she said as she consoled me.

I regained my composure and asked her, "How did you know to come over?"

"Well, your number came through on the caller ID, but the phone only rang a couple of times. I tried calling you back, but your phone line was busy. I knew something wasn't right. Thankfully, your door wasn't locked," she said.

I thanked her endlessly.

"It's all good. I got your back, Tiff. Stay close to me. You don't have to worry about watching your back no more."

Not only was she my most trusted friend now, but she was my bodyguard. She told me to hang with her so everyone on campus would know I was protected. For once in my life, I had someone who was willing to fight for me and have my back. We already worked together, and she had taught me a lot about the work politics, how to perfect my work ethic and improve my academics. We began hanging out more, and she stopped by my dorm a lot to kick it and watch movies.

In late fall 2003, I was nineteen years old, and although it had appeared that my parents were reconciling, word surfaced that my dad had married my mom's ex-best friend, Sarah. My mom took it better than we expected and enrolled herself into the university I attended for the winter semester. I was irritated by my dad's actions, but I was glad my mother didn't go back into a depression.

Lilo and Stitch, an animated movie, ironically spoke to the feelings I couldn't articulate. The emotional journey of the main character, Lilo, mirrored a lot of what I'd felt as a kid. The relationship Lilo had with her older sister, who was also her caregiver, resembled the relationship Tyler and I had. Lilo's desire for an unbroken family and friends who accepted her matched mine. She longed for a connection and to be understood. She also used music and the arts to articulate her feelings. It was like a cartoon movie on my life, so when it came to DVD, I made Robin come over and watch it with me.

When the movie ended, it was discussion time.

"See how good it was?" I said.

"Shockingly, it *was* good. Stitch is a mess!" She laughed.

"But he was perfect for Lilo."

Robin didn't say anything, but a smirk appeared on her face.

"What? What's that look?"

She leaned in and kissed me on the lips. I was taken aback, and my loss for words and multiple eye blinks showed just how shocked I was. "Umm ..."

"Am I your Stitch?" she asked.

"What?" I laughed. *Did she just compare herself to the fictional monster in the movie we just watched?* I thought. Indeed, she had.

"Tiff, you're pretty cool. You're beyond cool. We have a natural connection, and I care about you a lot. I think about you all the time, and we just fit."

Still silent, I asked myself, *How does this work?*

"I won't hurt you like the dudes you've been with, and no one will hurt you again."

Protection was key for me. I'd heard those other lines before from other guys, so mushiness wasn't winning me over, but protection sparked my interest. I'd lived much of my life uncovered, unprotected, but Robin had my back every time I needed her, and I knew she also packed heat. I needed protection, and I didn't care who it came from.

"Let me think about it and get back to you," I finally said.

She understood. "Okay."

As she walked toward the door to leave my room, she turned around and went in for another kiss, this time, adding a gentle but firm hug.

I called my homegirl Dana over, who stayed a floor above me, to share what happened so she could help me process. I needed to get my head right. I didn't like girls, and I didn't even know *she* liked girls.

"Tiff, you didn't know she liked you?" Dana asked in disbelief.

"Umm ... no. Hence the conversation now, Dana."

"Girl, she been liking you since our first dorm. Everyone could see that. You see how she dresses, how she carries herself?"

My mind scanned through snapshots of Robin. Sure, call me naïve, but I had been a tomboy my whole life. I didn't know dressing in boy clothes alluded to lesbianism. I thought we were just tomboys, homies.

"Tiff, weigh all the pros and cons, and go with what your gut tells you," Dana said as she departed.

I pondered on Dana's advice. I had picked guys for good sex but with the same abusive characteristics of my dad or the player characteristics my brothers showed with their girlfriends. Plus, I still hadn't fully processed and measured the effects of watching my dad hit my mother in the name of love then quickly betraying her by marrying her ex-best friend after thirty years of marriage. *Are all guys like this?*

I longed for protection and safety. I wanted to feel love, and if guys couldn't treat me right, maybe a woman would.

The next day after work, Robin and I walked back to the dorm together.

"Okay," I said. "Let's try dating. I'm down."

She displayed the biggest smile, but as quickly as I'd said yes, she gave me a stipulation. She was already in a relationship with another girl, but it wasn't working out. She wasn't happy, but until she could end it smoothly, we had to remain a secret. On one hand, I was fine with the secrecy because I didn't want to be known as a lesbian. But on the other hand, I had a hard time embracing the fact that I would be a side chick—to a chick for a chick. To make it more obtuse, I agreed to this madness.

We masked our relationship as a close friendship. I didn't tell anyone.

I still liked guys, so I didn't know how to work through whatever this was, but I rolled with it. As we spent more time together, we discovered that we had similar tastes in music, sports, and clothing. She, too, had come from a domestic violence home, but her mom remarried, so she knew what my family was going through, which helped me a lot. It also gave me hope that my mom could also remarry and have her happily ever after.

We had a family BBQ at my mom's house, and I brought Robin home with me. Just two girlfriends kicking it with family, no big deal—until Mallory wanted Robin to talk to her boy. Robin was a pretty tomboy. Though she wore boy clothes, she didn't look anything like a guy.

"Aye, Robin, my boy Brandon wanna holla," Mallory said.

"I'm good," Robin said.

Mallory and Brandon had a side conversation, which resulted in Mallory watching Robin half the night. "So, why you don't wanna talk to my homeboy, Robin?"

"He's not my type."

Mallory took a sip of her drink and quickly yelled, "Ma, Robin and Tiff are dating!"

Everyone froze. Stunned, I didn't know how to react. *Really, Mallory? Did she really just out me?*

"Well, that's our cue to go," I said. I kissed my mom and Tyler, and we left immediately.

I didn't want to see the reactions or even get into the conversations surrounding my secret relationship.

"Mallory is a jerk," Robin said as we drove back to campus.

"Don't talk about my sister. I'll handle it," I said.

I didn't know how to handle it, but regardless of her obnoxious behavior, no one had the right to talk about my sister. Our car ride was quiet as I plotted how to fix this.

When we returned to campus, Robin went back to her room with her main girl, and I went back to mine. Tyler called me within an hour of being back in my room to tell me our mother had called our dad to tell him about the new path I was on. From my mom's standpoint, every wrong I did was his fault, so calling him and going off was a common occurrence.

"What was his response?" I asked.

"Girl, he said, 'She's not out getting pregnant. I see nothing wrong with it!'"

I was stunned. "How did Mom take it? What did she say to that?"

"Mom didn't know what to say. She hung up on him."

"Well, clearly, his perspective shocked her further."

"Yeah, clearly."

"Do you have anything you want to say to me, Tyler?"

"No. I know you still like guys. This is just a phase. You should call our mother, though. Love you, kid. Gotta go."

I breathed a sigh of relief. Tyler could totally see what this was and wasn't.

I eventually mustered up the nerve to talk to my mom after I let a few days pass to assure her it wasn't what she thought it was.

"Mom, we're just super cool, and I still like guys, so don't worry."

"I am very worried. I don't like it. She's taking advantage of you based on your age."

"No, she's actually helped me out a lot, Mom; it's cool, really. We're just close friends."

With my family on high alert and knowing or having an inkling that I was in a lesbian relationship, I put the microscope on my relationship with Robin and the true reason I was even in it. Though Robin had been a great support, did we need to venture down this path for me to get the support I was looking for? Was this relationship worth my family knowing and judging me, especially when I was the side chick? I knew my family had high standards for me, but my relationship decisions were showing that I didn't have the same standards for myself. I couldn't reveal to them I had benched my self-esteem for moments of satisfaction during a quest to heal and overcome my abandonment and validation issues.

12

Season Shift on the Horizon

IT WAS ONE THING for Robin to tell me she was in a bad relationship and getting out of it, but it was quite another thing when time was lapsing and she still hadn't broken up with her primary girlfriend. However, she had a list of demands for what I could and couldn't do when I wasn't with her and how I was to act in public when I was with her. I started to rethink my decision and redirected my focus on school and getting money, the two defaults I used when I didn't want to face a major issue.

I was always taught that education was our way out. I started majoring in journalism, but after the first semester, I didn't want to go through a newspaper to get my start and changed my major to psychology. I always enjoyed psychology in high school and wanted to try to understand the reason for my dad's behavior. I also wanted to go into clinical psychology after college to help those who felt they couldn't talk to anyone, especially those who were growing up in dysfunctional homes and being exposed to trauma. I knew that feeling too well. My minor was in communications.

Outside of my studies, I needed money. I knew my mother

didn't have it, and I refused to ask my dad. My mom and siblings had been solely dependent on my dad. He had raised us that way, yet I was determined to cut that string. I was on an island of self and believed strongly that as long as I had God, I'd be fine. I had come this far without my dad, so I didn't need or want my dad or his money now. He didn't get to reject and abandon us as a family then wave some dollars in my face and expect everything to be okay. No thanks.

I was advised to take out student loans to pay my way through school with enough left over to help Mom and me. It didn't seem like a bad idea. I refused to ask for help, although that didn't stop my dad from offering his assistance and dropping off money orders for books. He knew I was dating Robin, so he also gave me money to give to her for gas and car maintenance in an effort to keep her driving me where I needed to go. He was using my relationship with Robin as an olive branch to get back into my life. I begrudgingly accepted, but he couldn't say I had asked for it. My ambition drove my ego and my grades were continuing to improve immensely.

My mom started volunteering in the front office at Evangel Ministries, and she was a faithful volunteer. It was no surprise. She was the administrator for the church we attended growing up. She began making friends, attending church events, and slowly traveling. She was even pressing toward the dean's list in college, which was a huge accomplishment. She had also lost a lot of weight. She was presented with a job opportunity because she'd done such an excellent job as a volunteer in the front office. The church was undergoing a leadership change. The assistant pastor, Pastor Chris Brooks, was becoming the pastor, and they offered her the opportunity to be his executive assistant. I was excited for her. I knew she could do it. It was just the thing she needed for her new life. Her comeback was strong through Christ. She was receiving healing and had a renewed outlook on life.

My dad sold our family home right from under our noses. It was an emotional time for us, and we cried a lot as we cleared out each room and reflected on the memories, good and bad. It felt like the casket was closing, and it was the end of what was once our family. As emotional as my siblings and I were, my mother didn't break. She didn't appear to be saddened, at least in front of us. She got a new two-bedroom apartment and fell in love with it. It was her new start and new life. Her apartment faced a pond and had a beautiful view. She had peace, and she was excited about what was to come. She didn't have to keep living in a place that reminded her of so much pain and hurt. She embodied having peace beyond all understanding through her relationship with Christ.

I started driving her car a lot, and we were mending our relationship. Driving her car meant having to pick her up. Thursday nights were her late nights due to bible study. One Thursday night, I went to pick her up, and she wasn't ready. Bible study was still going on, so I took a seat in the back and listened to Pastor Chris Brooks teach.

"Keep God's truth in front of your eyes and ears. Rejoice in today and have an attitude of praise. Put off bad things and put on good things to experience God's peace. You experience God's peace by staying connected to Him in prayer. Prayer is what keeps us connected to God, especially in challenging circumstances. When your faith is low, this shows you God is God. Write these down. Important prayer takeaways."

Takeaways? I was impressed. I'd never been in a church where the pastor gave takeaways. I quickly grabbed a pen and paper from my purse.

"One: Prayer isn't just for moments of crisis. Two: It's a two-way conversation. Three: The primary purpose of prayer is to know God's will. A good prayer is not when we ask God for what *we* want only, rather when we ask God for what *He* wants. Four: Pray using scriptures. It is written. This is the secret to

114

getting every prayer answered, asking according to His will. Information without application leads to frustration in your life. It's not until you change that everything else changes and shifts."

His teachings were making me think, reflect, and meditate. The truth was I never really prayed. I prayed for the abuse to stop, and I prayed He'd strike down my dad, but that was it. I always prayed over my food and before tests. That was as far as my prayer life extended.

Once bible study was over, my mom was shocked that I was even sitting there. Heck, so was I, but he was outstanding. He taught in a simple yet engaging way. He was sure to give the full context of why the scripture he'd taught on was written and what was happening during that time to connect the meaning. He then applied it to present day and topped it with modern-day humor.

My mom introduced me to Pastor Brooks. "Pastor Brooks, this is my baby girl, Tiffany," she said.

"Hey," he said as he leaned in to give me a hug. "It's so nice to meet you. Your mom talks about you all the time."

"Oh, great. Nice to meet you, too. Thank you for providing an outlet for her here and making her feel at home."

"She's home, and we're happy you're here, too. Your mom tells me you're in college."

"Yes, I am."

"Well, let's set up some time to meet. I would love to discuss further."

"Sure, okay."

"Promise me you'll come back and visit," he said.

I agreed to come back with an awkward laugh. I internally panicked because I made a commitment and had to stick to it. I got into the car and asked myself, "What just happened?" I was big on integrity, so against everything inside me, I knew I had to go because I had given my word.

Shortly after that night, I was let go from the campus job where Robin and I worked together, and I declared war on my former boss. The lawyer inside me arose, and I felt compelled to fight any injustice I witnessed. My passion had started in high school but grew in college. My mother didn't have a voice, so I felt it was my obligation to speak up for anyone who was being mistreated in my presence, including myself. My boss had been mistreating me since I started, from showing favoritism, to assigning me tasks without direction and catching attitudes when I requested more direction from her, to having us cover the office while she took long breaks. I voiced my opinion, which Robin had advised against. "Office politics," she said.

Robin, a professor, an intern, and I were in the conference room laughing and having conversation when my campus boss dropped my transcript on the center of the table. "Maybe you should focus on your grades, with this type of GPA, instead of sitting around laughing," she said.

The room became abruptly quiet. I immediately rose from the table with my bookbag in hand and followed her to her desk, flipping her the middle finger as I walked out the door.

"You're fired!" she yelled.

I didn't expect Robin to come after me because she still worked there, and I didn't need her to. I knew my next steps. Her actions caused me to go after her career of ten years. I wrote a grievance and took it all the way to judicial affairs, student government, and, ultimately, the dean of students. She didn't lose her job, but she faced some consequences that let her know what I did and didn't stand for, and that liberated me. It showed me I had a voice.

No one had tried to hear my voice in the past, so this fueled my passion for justice even more. I developed an impeccable work ethic driven by ambition, and I had proven myself faithful. After working at that office, I gained experience and our family friend knew I needed funds, so she referred me to her job at a major hospital. I worked in the discharge planning department, assisting nurses with patient meetings and coordinating the patients' discharge needs. I had no degree, and I wasn't qualified for the job, but the nurses and staff loved me.

One nurse even took me under her wing as my unofficial godmother. She and her husband gave me spiritual nuggets and indirectly planted inside me seeds of hope and forgiveness. They helped me see that there's light on the other side of the hard times I'd experienced. Most importantly, she made me realize I needed to start going to church more consistently, not for routine, but because I needed a relationship with God to order my steps in life. She taught me that all churches didn't mirror the bad experiences I'd faced. She also played gospel songs at her desk, and the lyrics pulled at my heart strings.

It took me back to a feeling I didn't know I missed. I felt connected to those gospel songs. They reminded me of the good parts of my childhood. The good I remembered about church. She even invested in me by buying my books a few different times.

My mom was also in my ear about coming to church more consistently, especially with me getting a job at such a prominent hospital, doing the work I was doing with no credentials. God was showing me favor and ordering my steps the whole time. Though I had distanced myself from Him, He was still close to me and was still making provisions for me. His love for me never left. For the first time since the divorce, I considered committing to consistently going to church like I used to growing up. Too many pieces of the puzzle connected to God—getting the new job and even connecting with the nurse.

Robin took me to work every day because she had a car. She even drove me to classes. It was a great benefit of the relationship, but I didn't like that I had to keep depending on her for rides, especially since she was still in a relationship and had a laundry list of rules, all while her main girlfriend was side-eying me. I began saving my money to get a new car. I originally wanted an orange Pontiac Grand AM GT. However, I wanted a truck even more. I had my eyes on a Ford Explorer Sport Trac.

There was one thing I wanted from my dad—his Ford employee plan. I felt I deserved it, so I decided to call him, and he agreed. I had a deal already worked out with the dealership, and he only needed to give them the employee plan details. But typical for my dad, he changed my whole deal, including the car type. He put the car in his name and added me as a co-signer without using any of my money. That was not what I wanted!

He appeared on campus with a brand new 2005 Ford Focus. While I should have been thankful, I was filled with anger. I didn't want a Focus! That wasn't what I asked for nor the deal I'd setup. That was how he controlled my siblings. His name was all over their cars, and he held it over their heads. I was trapped. He didn't want me to pay the car note. He only wanted me to pay the car insurance, which wasn't even in my name. To add insult to injury, he'd put his wife's name on *my* car. I hadn't asked him to put his name on my car or the insurance and definitely not his wife, so I wasn't giving a dime.

I still hadn't forgiven him, but, eventually, the fact that I had a new car changed my mindset, and I got excited. The freedom of not having to depend on other people to take me around was invaluable. It also caused tension with Robin and me as it allowed me to strategically drive around and watch her and her main girlfriend from afar in stealth mode. Having a car gave me visibility and insight into things they were doing I otherwise wouldn't have noticed. Depending on what I saw, whether they were leaving a restaurant together, coming back from somewhere, or walking to Robin's car with smiles on their faces, jealousy filled my spirit. I would speed past them so Robin would know I'd seen her enjoying herself with her girlfriend, which was a blatant contradiction to what she had told me. The story Robin sold me about being in a horrible relationship and leaving her girlfriend was false, and it was clear every time I saw them out and about on campus. I was playing a part in hurting a woman to gain validation from another woman. This couldn't be the best life had to offer me. I didn't like who I was turning into after seeing them together.

Angry, I wanted my dissatisfaction to be known in a violent way. I contemplated getting into a fist fight with Robin for wasting my time, making her pay for embarrassing me and making me settle for room visits and matching my class schedule to hers all in an attempt to "spend time" while she was open and free with her main chick. The revelation of the truth infuriated me. I had invested my heart, time, morals, and even money into this relationship. I sent hateful text messages and blasted angry songs, only to be sweet talked back into the dysfunction. Sadly, Robin knew the trigger words to make me feel like I was enough. I had been in the unhealthiest relationships with guys and now a girl, and I didn't know how to get out. I'd lost so much weight from being stressed out that I was down to a size zero. Many days, I had no appetite and would cry myself to sleep.

I knew my relationship wasn't right. I craved a love without the abuse, without infidelity, a love without manipulation. I longed to be in a relationship that reflected the good parts of my parents' marriage and receive an unconditional, agape love like 1 Corinthians 13 describes. When there were no fights and arguments, my parents were the most fun-loving people to be around, from their cute cuddles, surprise gifts, and the on-the-spot love songs they sang to each other while cruising around the city listening to the soundtrack of their love. I didn't know what a loving relationship looked like outside of their commitment, and with their divorce finalized, I couldn't even use that as my model anymore.

I was ashamed of having a relationship with a girl. I was mad at myself for putting up with the role of a side chick from

the very beginning. No one outside of my main circle knew I was
in a relationship with Robin because everyone knew her main
girlfriend. They suspected, but there were no confirmations. I
also knew I didn't fit into the lifestyle. I simply wanted to feel
safe and loved, but I didn't want to face judgment from others.
Shockingly, I was met without judgment. My circle loved me
like nothing ever happened.

In a random turn of events, I ended up sharing a class with
one of the college's football players, Nathaniel. He and I were
grouped together for a project, and that's when the flirting
began. What started off as casual jokes about another classmate
or something our professor said led to us discussing similar
interests like food preferences, music, and family values. He was
a cool dude and his purpose would soon reveal itself.

On my twenty-first birthday, I got a flat tire on my off day,
and Robin was nowhere to be found. Nathaniel was the only guy
I knew close to campus, and I had his number from the class
project we'd worked on together, so I called him.

"Hey, Nate. I hate to bother you, but I have a flat tire, and I
can't reach anyone to help me. Are you on campus by chance?"

"I'm on campus, but I'm at football practice."

"Oh, my bad. It's cool. I'll figure it out."

"No, you won't because I'm leaving right now to come to
you. Where are you?"

"Nate! What? No, it's okay. Stay at practice."

"While you were talking, I put you on mute and told Coach
I had an emergency. I'm halfway to my car, so where are you?"

As much as I didn't want to inconvenience him, I was excited
and smitten by his chivalry.

"I'm on Huron, close to the McDonald's."

"Cool. I'll be there soon."

"Thank you so much, for real. I appreciate it!"

"It's no problem."

After a twenty-minute wait, he arrived. To my surprise, he

brought red roses and a mini-birthday cake from a local bakery. My heart melted. I had no words for the level of sweetness he was showing me. He gave me a big, tight hug.

"Happy birthday, beautiful!"

I was lost in his embrace. It had been a while since I was in the arms of a man, though sweaty from practice. I felt the bulge of his muscles tightly wrapped around my stick-sized arms and the firmness of his chest. As our hug ended and he began to inspect the tire, his smile was just as big as mine.

"How did you know it was my birthday? How did you have time to grab this stuff? I've been to Dom Bakeries; they aren't quick."

"So you forgot our Leo conversation in class?"

"Ooooh, I did!"

"Well, I didn't. I actually grabbed these before practice. I was going to try to come meet up with you at some point today. It's your twenty-first, that's a milestone birthday. Where's the party at?"

Laughing, I responded, "Well, I appreciate that you thought of me to do this. That's so crazy how I got this flat, and you were the one to come to my rescue."

As he pulled the tire off to put the donut on, he smiled and said, "Looks like we're written in the stars."

In the stars? Now that was corny but cute. A guy pursuing me respectfully—I could dig it.

"Where's the party at, though?" he repeated.

"There's no party. Just me chillin' in my dorm room. Birthdays have been difficult since my parents' divorce, so I'm just chillin'. Plus, my tire is flat, so the dorm room is where it's going down."

"Well, I'm free from practice. How about you drive back to your dorm, and I take your car to the tire place as a birthday treat?"

My eyes grew wide. "Wait, what?"

"Yep, this is happening. Let's go. I'll follow you over."

"Umm ... okay."

I got into the car dazed and confused. I was always a giver in relationships as a protective mechanism so no one could feel they could control me with money or gifts. However, it still would've been nice to receive some thoughtful gifts like Nathaniel gave me.

We arrived back at the dorm. He parked his truck and came to open my car door, holding his hand out for the car key. Just when I started to think of all the possible ways things could go wrong, he gave me the keys to his truck.

"If you need anything, feel free to drive my truck while I take care of your car," he said.

"Okay, Nate, why are you so nice?"

"You're a woman. I have a mother. Besides, you're good people, and I can't leave you stranded on your twenty-first birthday. You're too beautiful to have no help."

"Well, help on then, my brotha!"

We both laughed.

"Well, thank you. I'm going to take a nap, but my dorm room is five-seventeen in case you call, and I don't answer," I said.

"Cool. Get a good nap, Sleeping Beauty."

As I walked back into my dorm, blushing and smiling, it was as if Robin didn't even exist. *Robin who?*

When I unlocked my dorm room and entered, my phone rang, and sure enough, it was Robin.

"Hey, apple head. Happy birthday!"

It was mid-day and I was just now getting a phone call. *She's got to be kidding*, I thought.

"Thanks."

"I saw you called earlier, but I was out taking care of business, and you know how that is."

She didn't have any business, except being with her main girlfriend.

"What was up, though?"

"Nothing. It's taken care of. I'm actually about to take a nap." I knew she had been unavailable because of her girlfriend, but it was my birthday; she should've made something up. I was over it.

"You okay? It's your twenty-first birthday."

"I'm trill, just want to go to sleep."

"Well, okay. I love you."

I hung up. As much as I wanted to turn off my ringer, I couldn't because Nate needed to be able to contact me about my car. Instead, I decided to drown out the ringer, so I could use the excuse that I didn't hear the phone.

The first track that was up on my birthday "over-it" CD mix was Keyshia Cole's song, "I Changed My Mind" followed by "Thought You Had My Back." I let that one play on repeat for a while as I sang my heart out like I was auditioning to be in the next music video. I then switched it to Destiny's Child's last album, *Destiny Fulfilled*, "Is She the Reason?" followed by "Through With Love."

During my when-a-woman's-fed-up-and-scorned concert, I heard knocks at the door. I peeped out the door to see what appeared to be a freshly showered Nate standing there; he wasn't wearing the same sweaty football clothes he was wearing earlier. I went to turn off my music and ran back to the door to let him in. Sure enough, Nate was there with Applebee's for dinner and the scent of freshly applied cologne.

"Sooo ... You showered at the tire place?"

"Nah." He laughed. "The tire place is around the corner from my place, so while they worked on your car, I walked home and cleaned up."

"I like how you think."

"Well, I try."

"How much do I owe you for the tire change?" I asked as I pulled my checkbook out.

"Nothing."

"What? Come on now, Nate."

"You ran over a nail; it was a quick patch job, and it didn't cost that much. It's my birthday gift to you."

"Bruh, you don't even know me like that to do all this."

"Well, from the sounds of the concert you were having that I could hear in the hall, I know you don't deserve the experiences you've probably had, and it takes nothing to be a friend."

I was speechless. No guy had been that caring and sweet. I decided to let it go and just go with the flow. "Well, thank you so much again."

"Okay, here's your food. It may need to be warmed up with all this talking you've been doing."

I laughed. "Do you have plans?"

"None at all."

"Wanna stay and watch movies with me?"

"Of course."

He felt like hip-hop to me, so I thought, *Why not watch* Brown Sugar, *and maybe I can get some sugar by the end of the night.* I could totally love him. He was husband material.

As we were watching the movie, there was a knock at the door.

I went to answer it and looked through the peephole; it was Robin. I eagerly opened the door.

"Hey, what's up?" I quickly turned around, walking away.

"Happy birthday. Why are you giving me a dry what's up?"

Robin walked further into the room. When she saw Nate, she froze. I knew she was angry, but I also knew that, as angry as she was, she couldn't show it because it would confirm the rumors that we were a couple. She couldn't have that because word would get back to her main girlfriend.

"Oh, my bad. Didn't know you had company. Y'all go ahead," she said.

She quickly left. I internally smiled and didn't attempt to chase her. "Back to the movie, shall we?" I said to Nate.

Shortly after her exit, my phone rang, but I refused to check it. About an hour later, when the movie went off, Nate left, and I finally checked my phone.

There was the text message from Robin: *I'm not about to play these games with you. You wanna cheat in my face, go ahead and be with your football boy. We're over.*

Cheat? How was it cheating when she had a whole girlfriend who lived in her dorm room? I felt liberated. I could continue seeing Nate. It felt good to not have to hide who I was dating anymore, to be dating a guy again. There was nothing like the strength and width of broad shoulders, a deep voice, and a hypnotic fragrance.

After my birthday, Nate and I went out on dates and rode to classes together. I was enjoying the dates and going to his football practices, only to find out a month later that he was getting back with his girlfriend of four years. They'd recently broken up when we had our class together, but they reached a resolution and decided to give it another try. Well, he served his purpose. He was who I needed to break myself free from Robin.

With all the ups and downs I'd encountered in relationships thus far, I decided I needed a break from dating to focus on my last couple of semesters.

13

Angels in Disguise

I HAD PNEUMONIA AT the top of 2005 and had to stop working at the hospital, but thankfully, after recovering, I rebounded with another job as an assistant childcare teacher at a daycare center that provided early education programs for preschool kids. I met a couple whose son was in my daycare class. They were a friendly black couple in their early thirties. With ongoing conversations about their son's activity in class, and because he was the star student, we had an instant connection. One evening, as they were picking up their sons (they had another in a different class), they offered to pay me to babysit the boys on the weekend so they could have date nights, and I agreed. I wasn't doing anything else. My job was down the street from my mom's house, and they lived about fifteen minutes from my mom's place, so it was convenient. They were my definition of black excellence with their faith, personalities, successful careers, family values, their home, and, most importantly, the love they showed each other in their marriage. I hadn't had a model of a young, black, successful Christian couple filled with love prior to meeting them. The closer I got to them, the more I shared my growth struggles and even my hesitations about going to church consistently. In all our talks, they motivated me through their faith and lifestyle and encouraged me to plug back into church, too.

It didn't take me long to notice the theme. This was more than a coincidence. From the nurse at the hospital, to my mom, and now this couple, I was being directed back to church. One of my observations from growing up in church was when people got into trouble, they went to church. Maybe they knew something I didn't, something I needed to tap into.

After being in these draining and toxic relationships, I felt consistently down in spirit, but I could hear their voices echoing the same message: *Get back into church.* I finally listened to the trusted voices in my life. I needed something more. But first, I needed answers to my questions about my dad because that's what was blocking me from getting back to church.

One of my memories from my childhood was of our family going to a church that was close to my college campus. I felt the urge to drop in and visit midweek to talk to the pastor. He was one of the sweetest pastors I'd ever met and truly loved our family. My parents tried marriage counseling once, and it was with this pastor, and I remembered overhearing the argument when my parents returned because this pastor had sided with my mother. He boldly told my dad he was wrong during their counseling session. My dad didn't agree and cut all communication with him, and we stopped visiting his church. Because of his bravery, I felt confident and trusted my instinct to have a conversation with him.

I walked into the church, and it felt like I was thrown back in time with flashbacks of the Sunday afternoon services we'd attended as a family. I remembered the laughs, hugs, smiles, and the good food the church provided. The pastor wasn't expecting me, so I was nervous and curious if the church secretary would allow me to see him. As I looked around in wonder at how well the church still looked, he appeared with arms wide open.

The hug was symbolic and paternal. I felt like a little girl running to the arms of my dad. I couldn't talk because the tears had taken over. He never shushed me to stop crying; he just held me and said, "God sees. He knows. He cares."

I needed that hug. I couldn't recall the last time someone took me in their arms and genuinely embraced me without judgement, prejudice, and lecture. It was evident I'd been bottling stuff up inside me as the tears poured.

He was patient with me as he walked me into his office and handed me a box of Kleenex. As I wiped my face, I told him the reason for my visit.

"I wasn't planning on doing that. I apologize," I said.

"Don't apologize. It's so good to see you," he said with the brightest smile.

"Well, I'm here because I need help and guidance. As you know, my parents are divorced. My dad hasn't changed, and our family is broken. I keep making horrible life decisions, picking the wrong relationships. I feel abandoned and angry, and I feel like I need to get back into church sooner than later. I don't know how I can get back into church. I hate my dad, and I need to know that all those years we were in church weren't fake. He was the preacher, the pastor, and look at the outcome. I just don't know what to do. I want to go back but need to know how."

"You all have been through so much. Your pain is real, and I empathize with you all. However, through your dad's imperfections, you still need to respect him because the Bible says to, and you can't harbor hate in your heart because it impacts you more than him. You can't understand it right now, but be okay with knowing that God will reveal the purpose. Just know God's intent wasn't for this. God will have the last say. You going to church isn't about going to church; it's about establishing a relationship with God that far exceeds going into that building, and your dad can't take that away from you no matter what he has done and do. I won't go too deep with you, but I'm going to give you two scriptures to read daily. Read

Psalm 46, The Passion Translation, "God on Our Side" every morning, and 1 Corinthians 13, The Passion Translation, "Love, the Motivation of Our Lives" every night.

"Okay."

I wanted to push back because I wasn't sold on the traditional belief that just reading the Bible would make everything better, but I trusted him enough to do it. I didn't question it, and I was obedient. I felt it was silly to read the scriptures daily but thought, *What could it hurt?* Maybe he knew something I didn't. It took months before I began to realize the importance of both.

The first scripture, 1 Corinthians 13, was teaching me unconditional love, that no matter what, I must choose to love. Psalm 46 was teaching me to have faith despite what I'd gone through and was still going through because God would handle it. Meditating on those scriptures daily was meant to help heal my heart. He was the first pastor to lay seed for my realignment. He gave me hope.

However, with the busyness of work and classes, I fell off from my newly formed routine. And although I understood what the scriptures meant, I didn't see things change immediately within my family, so I stopped reading them. I did, however, develop a deeper desire to be more committed to going to church so I could learn more about establishing a relationship with God the pastor spoke about and study the Bible more to get an understanding of the words on the pages.

One day while driving to work, I remembered I had an unfulfilled obligation. I'd told Pastor Brooks I'd meet with him. Honoring my word was big for me. I'd given my commitment, so I needed to fulfill it but not without a plan first. I had to figure out how to control the conversation. I didn't want to put on my fake face, but I didn't want to go too deep into all my issues with church yet. I was tired of wearing the mask of happiness to hide the pain, but I wasn't fully confident in going back to a place that gave me those flashbacks.

How can I be honest about how I'm feeling yet control how deep we get? I decided to go to bible study on a Thursday night. I'd talk to him briefly, and it would be done and over. He wouldn't have time to talk long because he would have just gotten done teaching. It was the perfect plan.

It wasn't until months later that I finally had time to go talk to him after service. I felt I had been bamboozled because there I was going to midweek service hoping to talk to him but couldn't, yet the bible study was good! The more I came, the more I desired to come.

Pastor Brooks' teaching was simple, practical, and profound. He answered questions I didn't know I had. The first night I attended, I purchased a notebook just for his sermons. I'd never taken notes in church before. I had professors for my college studies, and now I had a professor coaching me on a new spiritual growth journey.

One week, he talked about pain.

"Results proceed your thoughts. Stop remembering the pain of the past and being worried about what lies in the future. Don't let yesterday's problems steal today's joy. Remind yourself that pain is a part of life. You will have those few days that are full of trouble, but Jesus is a healer and deliverer. Pain gives birth to purpose. Without it, you won't fulfill your purpose. The purpose that pain serves is that once you go through it, it's for you to now help someone going through that pain. You're that person of hope now. Someone can say, 'Because of you, I can. Because you went through pain and made it out, I can, too.' Don't run just because pain is present."

I was taught that if pain was present, we were doing something wrong and God was mad at us. Pastor Brooks' teaching went against that theory by explaining that many people in the Bible dealt with pain and provided scriptural backup, and God resolved those pains, too.

The following week, he talked about how to get back to God if we'd fallen away or distanced ourselves.

"Many men in the Bible have walked away from a relationship with God. The scriptures show how they came back, and their relationship with God was restored. There was no condemnation, as His love never changes."

My curiosity was intrigued even more. Every week, his teachings were tailored for me.

The week after that, he talked about seasons.

"There are three seasons your parents never talk to you about. One: dry season—when you aren't hearing from God when you've lost your way. You've lost your happiness; you're not praying and just don't feel like doing right. Two: prodigal season—when you've lost your spiritual mind, turned your back on everything you knew was right. Three: faithless season— when you lose your faith because some form of devastation has ripped through your life, and you become angry and bitter because you feel like God has left you. When you do good but don't see it prevail."

I asked myself, *Is it possible to be in all three seasons?*

I instantly felt justified for blaming my parents. It was their fault! They didn't prepare me. I was subjected to their dysfunction and running into the arms of disastrous relationships. It was their fault my life was going in the direction it was going in. *I think I like this Pastor Brooks,* I thought.

But as soon as I found solace in placing the blame, Pastor Brooks went into his next set of points.

"The key isn't staying there and playing the blame game. You can get back after you've fallen through the road of restoration. Simply acknowledge that you've missed the mark. Acknowledge the season you're in and ask God for His grace and mercy."

Maybe I shouldn't have been so quick to place blame. *Is it really that easy?*

Everything I'd heard about being a Christian seemed overly

complicated and an unobtainable model of perfection that I clearly wasn't hitting. I was baptized at twelve years old, but I didn't feel any different afterward, and I was in a funk of shame and guilt because I knew I wasn't where I needed to be, but these sermons were reteaching me. Listening to his sermons, I felt like I was hearing the voice of God. Every part of the sermon that stuck out was God's specific details to me about what I was going through.

The more I came, the more excited I was to get a sermon from Pastor Brooks about overcoming, love, forgiveness, being a blessing to the family, the purpose and role of the family, finances, and reaching the world. He didn't teach from a place of perfection. What made his sermons stand out was that he delivered them as if he were having an informal conversation, and through his transparency and imperfections and sharing how he'd missed the mark, God's grace still covered him. He taught about how even though he desired to do what was right, he still made mistakes like Paul in the Bible. He didn't preach sermons that made me feel worse than when I had arrived.

At the core of his sermons was the message of the gospel, that no one was too far from God's love no matter where they were in life and what they'd done. I wanted more. He defied all my preconceived notions about the church, that everyone should be perfect and without flaws, and if you weren't perfect, you couldn't go to church or even be used in the church. Pastor Brooks was the first pastor who made me begin to change how I saw church, and he was the first pastor I'd ever known to coach us to prioritize having a relationship with Christ versus coming to a building.

He was about life change and challenged us to not just read the Bible for the sake of reading or hearing stories and quoting clichés, but to take the time to study it for ourselves and get a clear understanding of it, so we could apply it to our everyday lives.

He was just an everyday guy in his early twenties, trying to win over a generation for Christ. He was a college graduate, had a career as a financial advisor, and decided to follow his call of ministry. I was impressed with the fact that he was so young and decided to be a pastor.

As I waited to speak with him, I was rebuilt through these series of sermons. I learned more about his character, which developed my trust and helped me lower the walls of resistance I'd had for talking to him.

When we finally talked, it was months later. He'd finished preaching and surprisingly came to the back of the church for an impromptu meeting.

"Hey, Tiff!" he said.

"Hey, Pastor Brooks!"

"I'm so sorry we haven't had a chance to meet. Do you have a second?"

"Sure."

"How's everything going?"

I vowed to myself that I wasn't going to go into much detail about my life. "Going good," I said. "Working and ready to graduate."

He jumped right into the big question. "Why aren't you in church consistently?"

So, we're not going to ease into this, huh? Since he wasn't tiptoeing, neither would I. I cut straight to the chase. "My dad is a preacher and abused my mother and got away with it. I don't see how God could allow it. If God is so good, why did we have to go through that? I don't see how I can sit in service all day knowing my dad got over, and he's able to preach freely with nothing happening to him. My dad has scarred my view on church."

Pastor Brooks was silent as if he had no idea of what to say. He took a few moments to carefully choose the words he spoke next. I imagined he was saying a silent prayer: *Lord, help me with this one.*

"Tiffany, I'm sorry. I'm sorry your family went through that, and I'm sorry your mom endured that type of pain. The humanity of people is just that, humanity. Their humanity doesn't change God's divinity. Free will allows people to do good and do bad. God can't stop them from choosing, either. When you go back to the beginning of the Bible in Genesis to the garden when Eve ate the apple, that allowed a lot of the turmoil you see today to enter the earth. The imperfection of people started there. God's original design of perfection didn't have this. Make no mistake, God doesn't approve of your dad's behavior, but He uses both for His good. He doesn't condone or approve of that behavior; hear me clearly. God's model for marriage is for the man to love his wife as Christ loves the church as described in Ephesians 5:26-33. Nothing your dad did is right, and I understand that. The Bible lists countless stories of people who had family issues and personal issues, but when they surrendered to God with an unyielding faith, all those negative experiences worked for their good, Romans 8:28. This is going to sound crazy, but the distressing moments you've endured thus far were necessary for you to cultivate greatness from within. Be encouraged. Don't allow that to take your eyes off your relationship with Christ. Christ is the one who died for you, not your dad. He loves you with an everlasting love."

What do you say to that? I had nothing to say as tears fell down my face.

He gave me a hug. "You're my little sis. If it's okay, I'd like to keep checking in with you."

"Yes, that's fine," I said as I took one last wipe of my face.

"I also want you to meet my wife. You two have a lot in common."

"Sure, I'd like that."

I left, and on my drive home, I cried. I was thankful for the clarification and the revelation that there was hope. It seemed crazy that this was all necessary for me to cultivate greatness from within.

How is this going to work for my good?

The possibilities flooded my mind, but I was too drained to explore further, and crying took away any energy I had left. Thankfully, not much time passed before I had the opportunity to meet his wife.

One day, after getting out of class early, I popped up at the church to bring my mom flowers. Pastor Brooks was in the office when I arrived.

"Hey, Tiff. How are you?" he said.

"I'm good. How are you?"

"Good. I'm so glad you're here. You have a second?"

"Sure."

He walked me into the back of the sanctuary and told me to have a seat, and he went to his office toward the front.

When he came out through the double doors that led to his office, he was accompanied by his wife, Yodit. We sat and talked and had a great conversation. His wife had witnessed the same things with her parents that I had, and she used to have the feelings I had about her dad. I was shocked by her realness and transparency, and I was surprised that she, too, as a minister, cared enough to share.

Growing up in my prior church, the culture dictated that perfectionism was king, and we weren't to talk about family issues. Here, they were defying all the rules. Something was happening to me. My heart was softening. I embraced this change. I decided to start attending Evangel regularly for service.

Evangel had a concert series called Family Night of Praise featuring dance, choir, and drama. There was a dance concert in the evening called Jubilation, and it was nothing like I'd ever seen before. The performances were song lyrics illustrated in dance, beautifully orchestrated and choreographed. Thankfully, the song titles were on the bulletin, as I downloaded all of them and made my own CD afterwards. The church's worship department ministered to my soul. Because I'd heard so much preaching through my life, I felt God had to use another vehicle to get through to me and gain my undivided attention.

About two months later, they had their annual choir concert called Fill the Earth with Praise. Their introductory song started off sounding like a jingle, but when the choir began, it was the most beautiful sound I'd ever heard. The name of the song was "Lift Up Your Heads," and it was about three minutes long. I was speechless. It was a sound I'd never heard before. I'd heard some amazing choirs from my gospel records and church history, but I'd never heard a live choir sound so majestic.

The follow up song, "Oh Lord We Praise Your Name," sounded like a smooth, R&B ditty, and once the choir joined in, it was mind blowing. Their words were clear and harmonious, and the band was fire!

The choir director was the worship pastor, and I watched him in awe as he simultaneously directed the choir and band. One song after the other, it was an orchestrated work of perfection. In their rendition of Hezekiah Walker's "Jesus Is My Help," the electric guitar led. The choir took the song five levels higher. I stopped watching and began participating. I was up on my feet singing along. What I didn't know was I wasn't just singing the words to a song but making a proclamation over my life.

My expectations were blown away. I had been listening to lyrics of R&B and rap songs that identified with my story, but this concert played back-to-back songs that were seemingly written for me and gave me hope.

I started opening myself up and adding to my music collection a new wave of music in the worship music genre. It was different from gospel music. The gospel music I was used to was comprised of mainly choir songs with one lead vocalist. But praise and worship music could have a solo singer or just a singer with backups collectively focused on the admiration of God with a lot of exhortation and not a huge emphasis on singing.

My mom had a CD by Israel & New Breed called *Another Breakthrough* that I borrowed. The songs were affirming, from "Friend of God," "Friend," "Rise Within Us," "Breathe into Me," and "Breakthrough." I wore that CD out playing it so much. It was all I could listen to. I found myself crying to those songs, and I couldn't explain why, but I did know they were speaking to me on the inside. It was clear that I needed my sound to match this season of newness and harmonize with the direction God was taking me.

Between church and my mom in my ear, I slowly began to understand a relationship with Christ and what that looked like outside of the religious teachings I'd previously known. I thought I knew God, but I only knew *of* Him, the church building, rules, and its traditions. I began studying the Bible all over again to ensure I had the right foundation to view my experiences through the correct lens and experience Him, not just through the lens of my experiences but redefining my experiences through the lens of what the Bible said. The lens of God had a strategy even in my mess and mess ups.

14

Turn the Page

I BEGAN BLOSSOMING INTO a season of newness, the newness of a great job, growing spirituality, and my new apartment two buildings over from my mom's apartment. Though in this new season, my last semester of college started off rough. Financial aid was giving me the flux, the professors and I weren't seeing eye to eye, and my credits were mixed up due to changing my major.

Mallory shared with me her Donald Lawrence CD, and one of the tracks, "Restoring the Years," gripped me. It felt like it was God's promise to me. The next song, "I Am God," sealed the deal as it was a promise to me that no matter what was happening, God had me. Whatever I needed, He would be all of that and more. I played those two songs all day on repeat so much that the CD got stuck in my car's CD player. I had a new soundtrack to my life, not just sad love ballads and aggressive rap songs to further fuel my rage. I was beginning to feel like a whole new person with a new outlook to match.

At my new job, I had a coworker, Al, from St. Lucia who was so fine. He reminded me of Taye Diggs' character, Winston, from *How Stella Got Her Groove Back*. We casually flirted on the low while at work. He met me outside one evening as I was walking out.

"Hello, beautiful," he said.

"Hey, Al!"

"I would like to take you out this Friday. You have plans?"

"I don't, so sure."

We exchanged numbers, and I recommended a creole restaurant about fifteen minutes from my new apartment. I was so excited. It had been a year since I dated, and he was such a sweetheart. We talked for hours about our pasts, his daughter, his journey here, and our goals. But what seemed like what could have been a picture-perfect relationship was quickly tarnished by red flags that went off quickly.

He began talking about marriage instantly; though romantic, it was too fast. I even met his daughter. He became possessive and had obvious insecurities that I tried to look past because he was so cute. He was adamant about being sure that I was into him only and no one else had my attention. His possessiveness and controlling tactics became much more evident as I talked to other male coworkers.

He often accused me of flirting with any guy at work I had a conversation with. While sharing our pasts initially, I'd told him about Robin, and though she and I weren't together, we remained cordial and still had a few classes together, so we chatted occasionally. That posed a problem for him. I didn't think anything of it because I knew nothing was there.

One day at work, I was sitting at my desk laughing and talking to my coworker, Jason, when Al became aggressively loud with me, and I was terrified.

"Oh, so you're going to keep laughing out loud like that. Jason can make you laugh, huh?"

His tone was terrifying. No one at work knew we were dating, and here he was being extra, about to blow our cover. I turned around in my seat and looked at him like he was crazy.

Upon turning back around to my computer screen, I received an incoming email alert from him:

> *I mean you no harm; however, I am very saddened by the fact that you treat me as an enemy and flirt with Jason like this. I regret we happened. Nothing was supposed to be like this. I realize I've become public enemy number one, and I have vowed to leave you alone. I have vowed to leave the country as soon as possible, as this is too much for me. I see that Jason was able to fill the void of what I was supposed to be in your life. This will be the very last thing I send, as I am a proud man, and I will not humiliate myself, but you did not have to do what you did. I now realize how young you are, and I made a mistake getting involved. I hope to get out of the country as soon as possible as this place is now a source of pain and suffering to me.*

I didn't know how to respond. I had observed my dad's violent reactions frequently and saw how he misconstrued the smallest gesture like eye contact my mom had with another man, even if she had cordial conversation with him. My dad turned nothing into something, so Al's behavior raised a big red flag.

The night prior, he'd told me I was a horrible girlfriend because Robin called, and I talked to her while he was at my apartment visiting. He thought our friendship meant I still wanted to be romantically connected to her and, obviously, his anger rolled into the following day.

First, Robin, now this. I had a hard time comprehending how he could get to such an extreme in a matter of seconds, but I refused to entertain his behavior at work. Thankfully, he had to leave because he was an on-the-road computer technician, which required him to be offsite a lot for his job assignment. As soon as he left, I turned to my coworker and played it off. "What was that about? He's crazy," I said to ensure there was no indication that we were dating.

It was time to get off work. I grabbed my things and proceeded out of the building to begin the seven-minute walk to our assigned parking garage from the building we worked in. As I moved onto the sidewalk to cross the street and enter the parking garage, I was on my phone, telling my friend Sophia what happened at work.

He popped up out of nowhere. "You thought I forgot? You on the phone with your girlfriend, Robin?"

"What! You're being absolutely crazy right now, Al!"

Jason, thankfully, wasn't too far behind and saw what was happening. "Hey, Al!" he called out.

As Al turned to look at him, I ran up the stairs of the parking structure to my car while still on the phone with Sophia. From the yells of obscenity that flowed from his mouth, I knew he'd quickly realized I ran away. I wasn't 100 percent sure, but I felt as though he was searching the floors in the parking structure for my car. Though on the fourth level, I was grateful I could run pretty fast and skip steps largely due to my former basketball days. I jumped into my car, started it up, and pulled out of my parking spot quickly.

I saw him on the second level, and that's when my led foot came in handy. I sped through the structure, risking hitting other cars. Out of breath, I took a route I normally didn't take. Sophia wouldn't hang up and heard everything. She advised me not to go home right away and to meet her at the college library.

I met Sophia at my campus library, and we hung out there for a while before getting a pizza. She told me to follow her to her place so she could drop her car off, and she would ride with me to my apartment and stay with me for the night. So we dropped off her car and things. She grabbed an overnight bag, and we drove two buildings over to my place. I had no idea the level of crazy that was about to show up when I got home. As she and I walked up the stairs to my third-floor apartment, Al pulled up. I heard the car door slam as he parked in the middle of the street blocking the crosswalk. We turned around midway to the third floor and looked back at what was happening.

"You're just like all the other whores I've dealt with but worse! You cheat on me with a white boy in my face! I f***ing hate that I brought my daughter to meet you. You are worthless. I don't ever want to marry you. We are over!"

I was frozen, trying to comprehend his insanity. Sophia snapped me out of it by yelling at me to hurry up and get inside the apartment; he was making his way to the steps. We ran up the remaining flights of stairs and barely made it inside before he tried to push his way in.

"Open the door! Open the door, now!" He banged on the door.

I put a chair to the door and watched out the peephole, and Sophia called the police.

The neighbor across the hall from me came out of his apartment to confront him.

"She doesn't want to be bothered. I have kids here trying to sleep. Can you leave?"

Al silenced himself and turned away from the neighbor, facing my door again. He punched the door before walking down the steps. We ran into my bedroom to look out the window facing the parking lot. He began speaking in another language, so it was hard to understand what he was saying. Suddenly, he pulled his pants down, removing the boxers I had bought him, and threw them on my car.

"You broke my heart! You give these to your next boyfriend who you were flirting with at work."

We could hear the sirens coming closer, and he jumped into his car and pulled off. It felt like a scene from a Lifetime movie. The police pulled up, and Sophia called my mom as I spoke to the officers. My mom made sure I filed a personal protection order and alerted my boss. My job needed to investigate, so they put me on leave as they went through my emails and reviewed text messages to assist the police.

My boss was disappointed in me. I had an excellent reputation at the job and involving myself in an office romance was not a good look, especially one that was now filled with drama. I was terrified to go home and stayed with my mom during the investigation. Police paid him a couple of visits to warn him to keep away. The job let him go, and I was free to go back to work, but I was still afraid.

I was rethinking my entire life. I was horrible at choosing relationships. But I couldn't let myself stay too down because I had one and a half months left of school, and graduation was looming. I had to write a paper that determined the weight of my grade and whether I graduated. I had a broad imagination, but for the life of me, I couldn't decide what to write about.

Sophia encouraged me to write my life story. She was convinced I had a bestseller on my hands, so I took her advice. It was a raw and angry version of my life's events thus far. I hadn't yet healed, so I wondered how my professor would grade it. To my surprise, he loved it, and I passed the class.

Two weeks before graduation, my dad wanted to get me a graduation outfit. I was healing spiritually, so I obliged. He surprisingly bought me a beautiful red suit, and I loved it. I had stopped perming my hair months prior, so it could grow and hang low beneath my graduation cap.

Graduation day arrived. As I put my cap and gown on, it felt surreal. The odds were stacked against me since I had stepped foot on that campus, but I made it. I was so excited. Sophia was my right-hand woman, and she created my graduation playlist. I needed that playlist because I didn't know graduation day would turn out to be horrible, much like my high school graduation.

After getting ready and arriving at my mom's house, the vibe was off. She wasn't in a good mood, so I left to ride to the convocation center with Sophia. My mom arrived with Mallory. We hugged, they said congrats, and we moved things along. It was time for me to disappear and go line up with the other graduates. My good friends, who stayed across the dorm from me freshmen year of college, were graduating, too, so I joined the line with them so we could sit together.

When we emerged from the underground tunnel, I looked to my left and saw that my mother was visibly upset. She, Mallory, and Sophia were four rows from ground floor. *Why is she frowning? What's going on?* I thought. I had no signal on my cell phone, so I couldn't text Sophia to see what was up.

I felt the irritation rising. *Here we go again.* It was my day, and she was causing drama.

"Tiffany," I heard to the right of me.

I knew that voice. There was only one baritone voice that could call my name like that—my dad. When I turned to the right, there he was with his wife and my grandparents. I quickly understood what my mom's problem was. I knew, from that moment, the remainder of the day was going to be miserable.

My mother was mad and sad, and I watched her shrink into herself right there in her seat. This day was no longer about me; it was about them. My heart sank. This was my mom's first time seeing my dad and her ex-best friend together in public at a family function. I became distraught because it was my day and, yet again, it was ruined. My feelings of excitement had transitioned to just wanting the day to be over. Surely, nothing good could come from the rest of the event.

I sat through the graduation anxious and constantly looking to my right and left to monitor the looming shenanigans. I don't remember much of the ceremony because I was indirectly playing mediator, ensuring nothing jumped off.

The time arrived to line up to have my name called. As I stood in line waiting to hear my name and walk across the stage, I heard, "Go, Tiff!" The voice was familiar, but I couldn't make it out without a face. As I looked into the crowd, I spotted Pastor Brooks waving. He'd left church early to come to my college graduation. My eyes were filled with instant tears.

Once the graduates were dismissed and we went to our families, I saw him standing with my mom, Mallory, and Sophia, and at that moment, he wasn't just a pastor anymore—he was family. I never realized my faith community, including the head of the church, would take the time out to be there for me. That day, my whole outlook on God and the people in church changed. Someone had thought enough of me to choose me. Someone had taken the time out to celebrate me. He didn't know me that well, yet he took time away from the church to support me on a day that was spiraling downward and brightened it up.

I saw Christ's love for me through Pastor Brooks. I decided to join the church right after that, and my heart became open to experiencing even more changes for the first time. I wanted to grow deeper in my walk with Christ. I wanted to learn more, be more, and do more.

I went headfirst into my hunger for the Bible. I also began working a new job, making even more money. I needed it. No more classes, so I could grind full-time. The job wasn't in my career field, but it was okay for the moment. I wasn't dating; I was too focused on learning more about the Bible and developing my walk in Christ. I even began to slowly gain friends at church. I was enjoying the new Tiff, Graduated Tiff, Working Tiff, Adult Tiff.

Domino's Pizza recruited me to start my new career six months after graduating from college for an IT position. I wasn't in IT, but I was pretty tech savvy, so I told Walls, the hiring manager, I was up for the challenge. The next day, I received the call and was hired for the job as a temp with the opportunity to go permanent. I was shocked that they hired me, but I decided to maximize the opportunity and get a permanent spot with the global brand. I took every opportunity I could to go above and beyond. I created recap documents at the end of the week to show the progress from where I had started at the top of the week. I created documentation to explain my methodologies for what I was executing. I took initiative to take on more work than what was already assigned to me. Within two weeks, Walls was impressed and told me he would do everything he could to bring me on full-time. He was a man of his word. Three months later, he brought me onboard with a salary and benefits. He'd seen something in me that I hadn't seen in myself, and he gave this kid a chance.

I was a fast learner and quickly advanced with different projects. I was the youngest on the team, so I was the object of many jokes about my age, and unfortunately, true to my age, I threw tantrums that weren't becoming in a corporate environment. I didn't know how to manage conflict with coworkers and felt I could blatantly ignore them and show them with nonverbal communication how displeased I was with something they'd done. When Walls did something I didn't like, he was greeted with an attitude, given the silent treatment, and I put on headphones to mute him. He showed extreme patience by not firing me on the spot. Walls was a great leader. He desired to know what drove me and what my family life was like. Feeling comfortable with him, I overshared. I brought my family drama and mood swings to work, and it impacted my performance. I answered family calls and would be so wrapped up in their drama and emotionally invested that I wasn't concentrating on my work.

The tasks I was executing had high visibility as I was pushing down data to 5,000 stores, so quality assurance was of the utmost importance. It became a predictable cycle—Every time I had a family problem, it was reflected in my work. I'd have an issue when something was pushed down wrong or misspelled all because my focus was thrown off. If I could mentally detach, it would've been done right. Walls was secretly observing and stayed late with me one evening to have a conversation.

"Tiff, what's going on?" he asked.

"Nothing much, cranking this work out."

"Tiff, your displeasure with me this week has been pretty obvious. I have to be able to provide constructive feedback to you without you avoiding me, not talking to me, etc. Part of business is taking feedback from your supervisor, processing it, and moving on. If I gave our EVP, Chris, the cold shoulder every time he gave me non-favorable feedback, we wouldn't talk. And he'd probably get even more frustrated that I was acting the way you act toward me. If you don't feel you can work in this environment, let me know. I want to do what is best for you, and if another team in the company would better suit you, I will help you get there. I just can't continue to have you act this way toward me every time I provide some tough coaching."

Fear filled my heart. I couldn't let the one great thing I had slip through my fingers.

"It's not my intention. Each bit of constructive feedback you give me, I appreciate, and I try my best to grow from it. I appreciate all you have done and have taught me so far and would like to grow more on your team. When I receive any ounce of coaching, I take it as a moment of processing and getting re-focused and re-shift the expectations. For me, it means the bar has been raised another level. I don't ever want you to get the impression that I'm not working hard enough or I'm dropping the ball, so I go at my work full throttle. Then there's also, well, my family drama. My parents divorced, and we're pretty much a broken family in a lot of ways."

"I'm sorry to hear that, but you have to separate that from here. It's showing up in your work. Create some boundaries and allow this to be your sanctuary where nothing gets in. You have great possibilities and can do amazing things, but not at the rate you're going."

"Understood. Thank you."

"Anytime."

After he walked away and packed up his things, he came back to my desk before leaving. "Remember, it isn't your cross to bear. Every day, make the choice to leave that cross at His feet."

I had no response but to smile. My boss had just quoted scripture to me, Matthew 11:28, in fact. After our conversation, I got my act together and exceled at work. Walls gave me a developmental move from associate to coordinator within the year with more pay and more duties.

I was now managing the day-to-day communications, billing, and reporting for our department. I was one of the main communication conduits between our department and its respective internal customers. While my performance was peaking at work, I also began volunteering in the church as the armor bearer for Pastor Brooks' wife upon request; then I joined the youth department. This church introduced so many principles and biblical foundations to me that I'd never known or understood. I learned that everyone was created with giftings and purpose and got insight into what my spiritual gifts were.

"Tiff, do you know what your spiritual gifts are?" Yodit asked me.

"Um, no. What is it, and how do I find out?"

"Spiritual gifts are a source of happiness in your Christian life, and they influence your motives. It's a divine calling with divine responsibility because this is what God has gifted you to do. Go to churchgrowth.org, do the assessment and let me know."

I obliged. I answered the questions and discovered that my dominant spiritual gifts were showing mercy and administration. I dug deeper into what that meant. My gift of showing mercy meant I had the Spirit-given capacity to serve God by identifying with and comforting those in distress. I understood, on a deeper level, needs that weren't easily conveyed and was able to say the right thing at the right time to bring comfort and peace to others.

People gifted with mercy were also great counselors. This was a lightbulb moment for me as I became drawn to psychology later in my high school years, and it was a big focus, as my minor in college was psychology. I could pinpoint when this gift began to appear in my life, mostly with my mother as I was growing up, and I desired to be the voice for people who were going through a hard time in life and provide an ear for those who needed to share their heart and feel heard.

My second dominant gift of administration did not come as a surprise. The Greek translation is "kubernesis," meaning one who steers a ship, one who takes charge and puts the plan on paper and takes the leadership spot. I've been given the Spirit-given capacity to organize, administer, promote, and lead various affairs. I could see this gifting present since my younger years in church and home, which also connected the dots for the jobs I'd had as well.

Coming into the knowledge of these gifts made my heart smile. All this time, I felt one couldn't be used by God unless they were a preacher like my dad. However, that wasn't true. I played a role in His Kingdom. My giftings showed the light of Him working within me.

What now? I thought. It became easier to trace the hand of God all those years in His development of me and the underlying cause of some of the passions I possessed. It was why I had stronger feelings than others, but how did that shape my future? As soon as I asked the question, Pastor Brooks began teaching a series on how to use our spiritual gifts toward our kingdom dream.

"God wants us to dream because only with a dream to pursue do we have a reason to chase life. When we walk in our dream, things start to make sense in our life. God takes you through what you go through to position you for something better. Your purpose in life is your kingdom dream. It's what God will use through you to redeem the world. You can't determine it, you must discover it, according to Ephesians 2:10, as it's revealed through Jesus. You discover through seeking the heart of God by studying the scriptures, serving people in whatever capacity needed to drive out pride to test your heart, a heart to evangelize and dying to yourself, your wills and passions for Christ. It's bigger than you can do on your own. Lead people to Christ and be God centered."

I was discovering a tribe that was being drawn to me. Young adults who had grown up in dysfunctional homes like me and were being written off and mislabeled. I began mentoring a few young girls. I also began honing the gifting of administration more and took on more side jobs to dabble in entrepreneurship.

15

A Change on the Horizon

I WAS GOING TO church every week, listening to worship songs, continuing to excel on my job, serving in church—where I never thought I'd be—and trying to change a lot of my bad habits. So I was good, right? Wrong. Though New Tiffany was on the scene, Old Tiffany was on life support just waiting to be revived. While at the gas station in my hometown, I met a new guy. At first sight, he was fine. As I came out of the gas station, he was on the other side of the pump in his black F-150 staring at me.

His truck was as fine as he was, so I played it off, even though I was internally excited that someone so fine seemed completely awestruck and was staring at my beauty. I continued to the pump and began pumping my gas as if he didn't exist.

"Let me handle that for you, gorgeous," he said.

With my back turned to him, I smiled extra hard before turning around to face him.

"No, you're good. Thank you, though."

"Well, can I have your number and take you out? A gorgeous woman like you shouldn't be pumping gas, and since I didn't catch you beforehand, I'm obligated to make it up by taking you out."

"How do I know you're not a crazy guy?"

"I'm a mama's boy and just came from taking care of my dad. Here's my license with my first and last name. You can do a background check on me."

Derek was funny, but as hard as I laughed and even though I gave him my number, I remembered his full name from his license and ran it through the online Michigan offender search as soon as I got into the car. Nothing came up, so I figured this could be the start of something nice. Within two hours, he texted me with a proposed movie date for the next day. I accepted and was excited about his urgency. It had been eight months since my previous experience with Crazy Al, but I felt ready.

We went to the movies and dinner, and we had a lot in common, especially the fact that our parents knew each other. I thought it was a match made in heaven. He wasn't in church but believed in God. That was as far as he was willing to go. That was enough, right? I was determined to make him my trophy boo because he was so fine.

I was excelling in all other areas, except my love life, and, surely, I couldn't be thriving in a career without a good-looking man on my arm. We were going strong for a good month; then Derek began only calling me when he wanted me to come over at night or when he needed a bill paid. He then got bills in my name. He saw my corporate job as his benefit, and though I knew it wasn't right, I didn't want to walk down the road of yet another failed relationship, so I settled. As long as we could go different places and take a couple of pictures for my desk so folks could see how fine he was, I was good.

It became a sad norm for me. I picked my men superficially and kept receiving superficial results. The one good thing that was proven to be a great success despite my sad *situation*ship was my blooming career. After working with the company for almost a year, I was called into the office of the executive vice president for a conference call with the CEO. I was selected to receive the CEO Circle of Excellence Award along with six other people.

The other six people were managers, directors, and developers, and here I was, a coordinator, with a seat at the table. I was excited. I was thriving in my lane, and God was elevating me accordingly.

While serving Yodit as her armor bearer, I also jumped into serving the youth ministry. Knowing I had the gift of administration, I dove headfirst into establishing processes, notes, schedules, and getting programs on the calendar. Nevertheless, I didn't play well with others. This was an area left unchecked for some time along with my anger and defensiveness. These unchecked areas in a new world yielded a cycle of self-sabotage.

The summer of 2008 was filled with high emotions and pop offs. The smallest things set me off like I was the female Incredible Hulk. When I got mad, I didn't see red, I blacked out with anger. The rage in my soul turned me into a new person. I let little things build up versus addressing them head on, and because I'd get so angry, I couldn't see that it was overflowing into other things.

After receiving my award, I had to continue to work toward excellence. That meant continuing to draw boundaries and protecting my work time. When I was at work, I was at work, nothing else.

While still a newbie volunteer at church, I received an unprecedented amount of calls from my youth director, Pastor Avery, on my cell phone and desk phone, and he reached out through my work email, requesting that I be at the church shortly after getting off work with little travel time or breathing room. I allowed it initially, but after becoming aware that I was on the executive staff's radar I had to cease those interferences immediately. I sent an email to Pastor Avery to draw boundaries, and when he didn't adhere, I sent another email explaining that I was stepping down. However, I hadn't learned email decorum and how to filter my communication. I hadn't learned that even though I was conveying truth, it needed to be given in a way that didn't offend. My email was blunt, direct, and an attempt to put Pastor Avery in his place.

He sent me a follow-up email, praising me for my contributions. He apologized for his actions and took ownership for my concerns that led to me stepping down. He offered insight into our different styles and approaches to project management. But in the last paragraph of his email, he listed his achievements and accomplishments in comparison to mine. It was his hope that, when the dust settled, I could learn from him and gain beneficial tips from his leadership style.

His response led me to drive up to the church and confront him. I felt if someone was wrong, it was my responsibility to correct them. I was tired of people picking with me, and the little girl who was overlooked, mislabeled, and told what she was going to be had taken enough. After being bullied by most of the adults in my life, I was prepared to take off anyone's head if they stepped to me wrong. I was about my business, but I also realized there was another theme forming.

I found it a challenge to respect male leadership. They had one shot to stay on my good side, but the moment they did something to me, they were instantly crossed off the list. My interaction with Pastor Avery revealed this gripe in a deep way. I no longer respected the man who was once the leader of my house. I saw my dad in all of them, and it felt like a painful attack each time a male leader corrected me.

My visit was followed up by an email to the operations director and Pastor Brooks, and I even used scriptures to support my claims. I hated how my dad took one piece of scripture in the wrong context to validate his behavior and opinion growing up, yet here I was, in my mid-twenties, doing the same thing. I was wronged and no one could tell me I wasn't wronged, and because a church member was doing the wrong, I used church language to support me. I wasn't afraid of speaking about what was right and having proper documentation to back up my claims. I provided evidence via my call log, my increased phone bill, a documented trail of emails that came through my work email, and I even interviewed other youth volunteers to collect corresponding concerns—all stamped by scripture.

Amidst my church drama, Mallory and I had a bad argument. I picked her up from work, and she was being disrespectful, which caused me to drive 90-100 mph to scare her. I mainly wanted to get her home and out of my car. My driving terrified her to the point of her yelling for me to let her out of the car. I slowly pulled over to the shoulder on the freeway and let her out. She slammed my door as if she were trying to shatter the window.

I called my dad. I don't know why, but I wanted swift vengeance, and I wanted him to handle Mallory. The results were quite the opposite.

"Tiffany don't call me for this mess. That's between you two. You created it; you handle it."

My anger was at level 200 as I pulled into the parking lot of my mom's apartment and walked into the house.

"Don't call you for this mess? You created this mess!" I yelled at the top of my lungs.

"Tiffany who are you talking to?" my mom asked.

"You better watch who you talking to, young lady," my dad responded.

"I ain't gotta watch nothing. You never watched how you talked to Mom! You never watched how you treated her! It's because of you our family is this way. It's because of you I gotta take care of her now because if the abuse wasn't enough, you left her close to nothing. You treated her like she didn't give you thirty years of her life!"

"You shut the hell up right now!"

"Make me! I ain't scared of you. Everybody may be scared of you, but I'm not. I dare you to put a finger on me. I'm ready to beat your a** for what you did to Mom all these years!"

I was enraged as I changed clothes while he was on speaker phone. My mom tried to calm me down. She grabbed the phone, telling me to stop.

"I'm done with you. Don't ever call me for nothing!" he said.

"I've *been* done with you, and I can't wait until you die. I hate you! You're a mockery to the Bible, and I can't wait until God strikes you down!"

"You got a lot of talk there!"

"Oh no, I'm about action. Watch me pull up. Meet me at your mama house. I'm on my way." I hung up.

I felt liberated. All the resentment I held in my heart for how he'd treated my mom and his children came out verbally, and I now had a chance to show it physically. I drove to his parents' house and parked on the street. I got out of the car and sat on the hood wearing high-top Air Force Ones, basketball shorts, and a tank top, ready to fight my own dad. On my hip was the Smith & Wesson blade I'd purchased.

I was ready for wherever this fight took us. One thing I knew was that I wasn't going to be my mother. The flashbacks of him beating her down and her screams for help plagued my mind. I wanted him to pull up. I wanted to avenge my mother and our family. If no one else would do it, I would be the one to take this giant in our family down.

Suddenly, my phone rang. It was my grandmother.

"Tiffany, you need to go on home now. You're being so disrespectful. God is not pleased."

"Excuse me? You've never called me to even say hi; yet you call me to defend him? You all are the ones who created this monster, the whole family fears him and lets him be crazy without ever putting him in his place. Don't you dare tell me what I'm being when he's terrorized our family the way he has with no help or support from you all."

She hung up on me.

Tuh … God is not pleased. God is not pleased? They sure love to bring God into the equation when they need saving. Ain't they a trip?

I waited two hours, until it got dark, before finally leaving. I felt great, though. I had called his bluff, and he didn't show up. But something in my soul felt off, and there was a knot in my stomach.

Why do I feel this way if I won? I had finally done what no one in my family could do. I stood up to my dad on behalf of our family. I called my trophy boo to do what I normally did in high school when I couldn't process my feeling of emptiness. Sex would fix it.

It didn't, though. The emptiness was now coupled with a longing for more. I normally would spend the night, but that night, I wasn't feeling it. After I got out of the shower, ready to head home, I saw an alert on my phone signaling an email. I grabbed the rest of my things, walked to my car, and opened the email. It was from Pastor Brooks:

> *Tiffany, you are a very gifted person. Viewing the work you've contributed to the youth department has made me really emotional. I am so saddened by the recent events that have transpired. I have been praying for a long time that God would use you mightily because I realize the great call on your life. My heart is broken that the enemy has come in and prevailed at hindering your ministry from going forward. This is not how things were supposed to be. You must remember that "We wrestle not against flesh and blood." People aren't your problem or your enemy; Satan is. He knows that, because human beings are imperfect, he can always use them, but you must always avoid being tripped up by*

his tactics. If all you walk away with from this situation is the perception that Pastor Avery is a bad guy or a horrible leader, then you have missed the bigger point. There is much to be learned from this difficult situation on all sides and by all parties involved. I have challenged Pastor Avery concerning the lessons he needs to learn, and he has been very humble and willing to accept correction, but I pray that you will embrace your areas of weakness and immaturity also. Because if these lessons are not learned, all Satan will do is keep sending other people to trip you up, and you will miss out on the awesome things God wants you to accomplish for His glory. Yesterday, you sent me a detailed listing of all his failures, but I didn't see you provide me with an equally detailed list of your own shortcomings. The only way we grow is by being thoroughly honest about our own failures. I would like for you to submit this list to me because I know it will force you to grow. In addition, I would like for you to let me know who you consulted with before you responded to Pastor Avery's mistakes. Whose advice and guidance did you seek before you acted? Who did you have proof your emails before you sent them out? Finally, please communicate what your process is when it comes to addressing the failures of those who have leadership and authority in your life. What scripture do you use to govern how a follower should respond to the mistakes of their leaders? You quoted scripture in your previous email concerning Paul's instructions about order in the church. I fully agree with that verse, but I think there is one major point you have missed. And that is that followers and subordinates are not called by God to correct their leaders. When leaders make mistakes, they must be corrected by those who have authority over them. I feel that it is perfectly fine for you to share with me your concerns and disappointments or share them with the assistant pastor or operations director, but I don't feel it is your place to correct leadership. I would also like to know how much time you spent praying for the leadership of the youth department when you saw leadership weaknesses. Did you ever arrange for the team to get together to fast and pray for your brother in the Lord to help him become a better leader? Did you ever purchase him any books or resources on how to become stronger in the areas where he needs to grow? I guess what I am saying is that the easiest thing a disappointed follower can do when their leader makes a mistake is complain. All leaders have weaknesses and make mistakes; you will make your fair share of mistakes also. But the mature thing to do is empower that leader and help them grow. This takes patience and forgiveness and, most of all, an anointing from the Lord. I feel your approach in this matter was not handled with the best wisdom, and you should strive to ask yourself how you could have expressed your concerns in a more respectful way. Tiffany, I love you like my own flesh-and-blood sister. I would never allow anyone to hurt you without standing up for you, but I don't want you to fight unnecessary battles. I know this has been a difficult season for you, and I don't want you to feel that I am coming against you or trying to condemn you, but as your pastor, friend, and big brother, I want you to grow so you can have peace.

I looked up from that email and felt a heavy weight on my shoulders. I was still sitting in the car and hadn't put the key in the ignition. I was in a trance as I began to think about all the events that had occurred in the past seventy-two hours, from my run-in with the youth director, my sister, my dad, grandmother, and now this email from Pastor Brooks.

If I'd grown so much in Christ, why was this happening? I felt like I had hit a wall and couldn't recompose myself. I didn't know how to process the root cause of what happened or what was happening. I hated crying because I felt tears were for the weak. I was always told to hurry and wipe my tears as a kid to mask the pain; yet, in this new season, I cried more than ever. I felt weak and hopeless, but my pride wouldn't let me stay in that place.

Through all the words that were spoken over me and the things that had been done to me, I was the hurt one. I expected everyone to overlook my actions and give me a pass because I was the victim. None of this would have happened if my dad didn't beat my mom, if my mom hadn't snatched me from our home every time she decided to leave my dad, if they hadn't divorced after thirty years, if they hadn't snatched my childhood from me because of their dysfunction. As I backed the car out of the parking spot, I felt justified. I went to my mom's house to get a good night's sleep.

Pastor Michael Bonner, the worship pastor at the church, knew of me because he was friends with my mom. We'd had two conversations, and when the issues with Pastor Avery and I surfaced, he briefly counseled me on how to handle it. But I did the opposite of what he told me to do. By the next morning, word of my shenanigans got around, and I awakened to an email from him. As I read it out loud to my mother with my chest out, offended by his audacity to chastise me, my lips quivered, and the tears began flowing.

I couldn't finish the email. My mom took my phone and finished reading it as I cried. This was the first time I cried in front of my mom as an adult. I always tried to be the strong one for her, so I never allowed her to see my tears. She read the email out loud:

Hi Tiffany!

It saddens me that you did not listen to my advice. You agreed and consented with me that you would let this "drama" go, but you did not. What that means to me is that your word has little value. A person's integrity is in her ability to say what she does and do what she says. You did not.

Many people are impacted by this drama, those who love you and those who you have worked under or with. To be a good servant of the Lord and a servant of people, you must demonstrate a willingness to discipline yourself. For a true servant knows that the words that come out of your mouth come from the heart. If the heart is not rooted in the wisdom and Word of the Lord, as David said, "I hide Thy word in my heart that I might not sin against Thee," then the utterances are of "self." Instead of examining yourself, you have placed the spotlight and blame elsewhere.

Your attitude as of this writing demonstrates that you have not spent time in prayer or with counsel from the Holy Spirit. You are out of control and need to take the key out of the ignition and kill the engine. The true question is not how God will deal with them but how He will deal with you. My prayer for you is that you repent for all the things you have done and allow the Lord to purge you of all the bitterness, disappointments, anger, and frustrations that you have allowed to be in the driver's seat. Allow the Lord to extinguish the "little fire" of your tongue and be the pilot of your ship.

May His peace and love overshadow you so your walk in Him will be greater and produce the fruit of the Spirit in you of which others will be drawn to Him through you. ~ Love Ya - Pastor Mike

Mom called Pastor Bonner and explained to him the full picture of what occurred with me and the youth director, my sister, dad, grandmother, and how I didn't have the tools to process and handle conflict. He wanted her to give the phone to me because he wanted to talk to me, but I couldn't do it. My mom noticed something, though. She saw that out of all the voices and disappointing emails I had received, my reaction to his email showed a connection. She requested a face-to-face meeting.

We drove to his home in a wooded suburban area. As we pulled up to the circular driveway of their big house, I couldn't help but wonder what lay inside. I'd been a part of these so-called intervention meetings, dating back to the church group in 1994 that went horribly wrong, so I wasn't optimistic. Pastor Mike's wife, Sherry, opened the door. She hugged us and directed us to the kitchen. Pastor Mike was standing in front of the table with his arms extended for a hug. Hugs were nice, but I was skeptical. I wanted this to be over.

As we sat, Pastor Mike put his glasses on and read his notes. "Your mom has shared with me your story. You and I have had brief conversations. Your life thus far is very moving. Looking at your words and actions, they reflect those of someone who has been on a journey filled with pain, disappointment, and abuse. You've been on an endless ride on an emotional roller coaster to hell. That makes Sherry and I feel very sad. Thank you for sharing your experience with us. Thank you for sharing your pain, bitterness, and disappointments with us. We don't take that for granted, and it is our prayer that what has occurred will be a new chapter of redemption and restoration.

"I am so grateful that you were born, and part of your destiny was to be with me and Sherry. Though you may not want to acknowledge it, your birth dad had a part in bringing you here. There are some good memories you may have of him as a good dad. Keep those close along with the bad things he has done.

Just as sins can be forgiven, forgiveness is a choice that Jesus has encouraged us to make. Do what Jesus did. Though all men fail at some point in life, some men continue to fail all their lives. Know that the nurturing relationships of family teach us the values of love, sacrifice, strength, joy, sadness, justice, and peace. You have one! Though your experience with your blood family has not always been paradise, you do have a family, and your relationship with them continues for the rest of your life. Your interaction with them should include love, compassion, and forgiveness.

"The Lord did not leave you in an impossible life situation but has made a way for you to still be blessed with an extended family that embraces you. Your present anger and bitterness are understandable, and you have a right to feel that way. Even severe disappointment is a feeling you can embrace but only for a time. The Word says we can be angry, but sin not. It also says, 'Do not the sun go down and still remain angry.' I know how hurt you are and how it runs deep into your soul and spirit. You are wounded, and you want to retaliate or even destroy if allowed. The Supremes used to sing a song called 'Stop in the Name of Love.' I say stop in the name of love for yourself and your gentle spirit. Let go of the anger, bitterness, and resentment you have for your dad and those who remind you of him. These emotions are truly dangerous and will disable your ability to love, forgive, and grow in the grace the Lord has given us all."

My tears flowed nonstop.

"Your words have power. Like a sniper, you assassinate people with the things you say with no regard for the after effects."

I interrupted him and became defensive. "I'm not out here taking folks out. Why is it okay for them to say what they want to me and I just take it? I've been taking it for years!" I argued.

"Most of the time, when I am texting by phone, I use 'God's morning' as a greeting. The Word reminds us that 'this is the day that the Lord has made. Let us rejoice and be glad in it.' Most mornings, we all seem to be challenged with either the same routines or faced with a decision about what to do today. The road to an enlightened and successful life is paved with the many proverbs recorded in the Old Testament. 'Happy is the man who finds wisdom and understanding for the gain from it is better than gain from silver and profit better than gold,' says Proverbs 3:13,14.

"As an experienced person in life's unexpected winds of change and challenges, I have come to know that God's Word is true. What I've found, and maybe you can agree with me, is that wisdom too often never comes, so one ought not reject it merely because it comes late. As it has been said in a very familiar saying, hindsight is twenty-twenty.

"I commend you for all you've accomplished thus far, but you must bridle your tongue and your temper and keep your focus on Him, and don't let the obstacles of life keep you from reaching your goals and achieving your vision. You should write these keys down and meditate on them. Psalm 119:165, 'Great peace have they who love your law, and nothing can make them stumble.' Your key to freedom lies in your power to control your thoughts and tongue. If you are patient in one moment of anger, you will escape a hundred days of sorrow. Be not angry that you cannot make others as you wish them, since you cannot even make yourself as you wish to be."

I was silent. Going off on people and hurting them with my words was a defense mechanism. If someone went low with their words, I went lower to cut to the white meat. I had been hurt many times by people's words growing up, so it became my goal to avoid getting hurt again. The lower I hit, the tougher I felt. It was a classic case of "hurt people hurt people."

No one had taken the time to really tell me the effects of my behavior or how I could even grow. Surprisingly, it wasn't a Tiffany-bashing session. There was a light at the end of the meeting. The Bonners desired to become my godparents. They didn't want to just show me my faults, they desired to pour into me and help me overcome my challenges. They saw potential in me and a call on me that they felt was worth assisting. My new godfather said, "As a Bonner, you're protected. You have a covering. We trust each other, and we're there for each other."

I wanted all of it. Yes, I had my own family, through good and bad, but I needed an outlet because I didn't feel loved by my family at the time. My family was broken from the divorce, and we didn't know how to love each other again through the hurt. My parents' divorce didn't just happen to them; it happened to all of us, and they didn't see that until later. The lingering effects were debilitating. We didn't get along like we used to. A part of us died when the marriage died, and it took some of us many years to rebuild. The damage was done, and I was desperately in need of a change.

I hadn't seen this Christian walk modeled for me, and in the process of all my new learnings about Christ, I was still stuck with how to apply it all. With my new godfamily, we created a process of email check-ins, phone calls a couple times a week, and church attendance. I didn't want to attend church anymore after the drama, but Pastor Mike wouldn't allow it. He even went as far as to put me back into a leadership position under his department as the team lead over the visual services team. When he told me, I was irritated; I didn't want to do it.

"Why would you put me in this position? I just went off on senior leadership. Clearly, this isn't the fit for me. Don't churches put you out for what I did? And here you go wanting to make me a leader. This doesn't make any sense. Let me just fade into the background."

"Well, I want to keep you connected and close to me. So far, I've discovered you aren't as bad despite what has been said about your attitude and lack of respect. You just need to be understood and valued. I want to see how well you play with others."

"Play well with others? I go to work every day. I think I know how to play well with others."

"That doesn't mean you're truly successful. That could mean you know how to mask it. Your mother has confided in me, and I want to be a help. You need to be diffused from your anger, and this will allow me to see who you truly are and what's going on. This is an opportunity for trust, love, and the privilege of being able to sow into you."

"Privilege to sow into me? You actually like that you have the problem child? And this sounds a lot like an assessment."

He chuckled. "You're not a problem child, and, actually, yes, this is an assessment. I'm an auditor, going on thirty-five years. I want to understand and assess your skillset and your willingness to follow instructions."

I didn't want to, and it was hard, but I did it. To endure the menacing looks, questions, rumors, and gossip, I was faking it again and going to church as a routine, to get it over with. I dropped my trophy boo because, quite frankly, I was sick of paying all his bills. As fast as I dropped him, I began dating a new guy, Damien, who I used to go to church with when I was younger.

The church we attended when we were younger was the church my dad pastored, so I felt, of course, this was a good match. I was back in the church, and he had a church background, so it was meant to be. Damien was "the one." After a couple of weeks of dating, he took me around his family, and it was like the good church memories we had formed when I was younger. After a couple of months, I even took him around my family and brought him to the family reunion. We had goals and dreams, and before I knew it, I was unofficially living with him before marriage, thinking I was living the life. But it was short lived. I went through Damien's phone nightly and saw texts from other chicks describing things they'd done or recapping conversations they'd had. I would lay in bed and notice he wasn't on the other side. I'd listen to him tiptoe out of the room to sit on the couch and whisper on the phone to other women. I also crept out of bed to eavesdrop and confirm my gut feeling. After hearing the heartbreaking truth, I'd get back into bed, crying and asking the Lord why.

It wasn't uncommon for me to see Damien talking to other girls while we were in the club after he'd strategically sat me in the VIP section so he could flirt. I'd look down through the glass to the dancefloor and see him whispering in various girls' ears and exchanging phone numbers. After watching this happen too many times, I became fed up and decided to go down to the dancefloor to confront him and his selected girl of the moment.

With a shove in his back, I said, "Damien! You're bold enough to do this in my face?"

Clearly drunk, Damien turned around and rolled his eyes at me as I stared back with fire and rage. He acted like we didn't ride to the club together, like we weren't unofficially living together. Sure, I hadn't moved all my stuff in yet, but I stayed at his place for weeks on end. He was blatantly treating me like we weren't a couple. Suddenly, I felt some sort of liquid on my arm. I quickly realized the girl he was flirting with had tossed her drink on me. I tried to jump at her and reach for her to beat her down, but he picked me up and carried me out of the club. His cousin was with us, and we argued the entire way to his aunt's house. When we arrived at his aunt's house to drop off his cousin, he got out of the car. I quickly realized the girl from the club and her friends had followed us as they jumped out of their car.

I sat on the passenger side thinking, *Is this even real?* I made sure my door was locked as well as the passenger door to the backset. Damien just stood there with the driver's door open. I wasn't sure what was about to happen, so I unstrapped my heels. The girl from the club pushed him aside and jumped into *my* car through the open driver side door and was instantly met by my size-eleven foot to the face. As she shook off the blow, she came back, and I gripped her hair and slammed her head into the stirring wheel. One of her friends tried to squeeze into my car behind her through the driver side, trying to reach me. I threw more punches.

My boyfriend's cousin came outside and pulled the girls out of the car. The neighbors called the police, so the girls quickly left.

This was what my relationships had turned into. I was a corporate executive by day and club fighter by night due to my horrible selection in guys. A saying by my goddad came to mind: *"What you compromise to keep you'll eventually lose."* His words resonated with me as I reflected on my relationship.

When I confronted Damien, he used the lame excuse that I didn't trust him, and he couldn't be with a woman who couldn't trust him. He even grew angry and cussed me out for going through his phone. Here I was in another relationship that involved verbal abuse and cheating. I didn't deserve any of it, and he didn't deserve me, but I felt I had to keep compromising because I thought there were only so many failed relationships one was allowed to have.

The disrespect continued, and I stayed. I was miserable until one day, my aunt Jill picked me up for an auntie/niece day.

"Sweetie, now you know I love you," she said, "but you need to let him go. He talks to you and treats you like a dog, and you take it. Baby, you have family here who has your back. You don't have to settle for this. Who knows what the future could be, but you need to walk away and fast!"

I wondered how I ended up in that place. I had classified myself as the "wifey type," doing everything a wife did so I could get a ring, but I wasn't married. And as much as I wanted those guys to "wife" me, the reality was I wasn't ready to be married. I only wanted them to marry me because they were shiny and new. I was giving myself the role of wife and investing heavily into the relationship with no return. With all the disrespect and cheating, my self-esteem took a hit. I was trying to live up to society's standards but failing miserably.

I prided myself on being Ms. Independent and the "baddest chick," a force to be reckoned with, refusing to downplay my personality and credentials because it was who I'd become. But, unbeknownst to me, I was lowering my standards with every relationship. I didn't trust, didn't allow myself to be vulnerable, and I had to control everything so I wouldn't be controlled. I dated people who were as broken as I was, hoping they could fill the holes in my heart, when, in reality, they were filling my heart with their own unhealthy vices. I was my weakest while dating Damien. Ultimately, we were infecting each other.

I was dead set on not having a man like my dad, so I made sure to control the situation, which was me subconsciously acting like my dad, yet I was being manipulated like my mother. Feeling like I had to prove something and to keep myself from being controlled, I lent my credit, cashed out on gifts, and paid off credit for men like a complete fool, getting nothing in return, not even a birthday card. I still tried to be spiritually strong, so I thought dating guys who said they were Christian or loved God as a bare minimum was cool.

I felt I could fix them. Afterall, they said they were Christians. Appearances were big for me. I wanted to look like I had it together, like I could have a career and a man. And I still had a chip on my shoulder as I constantly tried to prove to people that I was who they said I couldn't be. As I pursued Christ more, the friction between Damien and I increased, and we argued more. He disrespected the church, criticized my commitment, but I refused to bend. I took Aunt Jill's advice and moved out, never looking back.

After the relationship ended, I made a re-commitment to Christ to stay involved, hold myself accountable to key folks

I trusted, and pour myself into serving the church. I needed to stay in the Bible and involved with ministry departments at church to keep me grounded and out of trouble. It was time.

16

Dead Ends

THERE I STOOD, BROKEN, standing face to face with myself. I was tired of that feeling. It was time for me to throw my manual away and stop driving my life. God has a funny way of showing you that you're not all that. While I thought I was all that and more at work, I was dealt hardships at work that my ego couldn't get me out of. The drama with my ex-boyfriend didn't resolve without residual effects. The mental impact had a way of showing up in my work, and, consequently, when things started getting rocky and my focus shifted from my work, my boss had to have another conversation with me to get me back on track, still with compassion and grace.

It was Memorial Day 2009, and I was at my apartment tossing and turning in my bed. I was so unhappy, and there was a heaviness on me like two-ton weights sitting on my chest. I sat up on the edge of my bed and dropped to my knees crying, feeling hopeless. While crying, I began praying.

"Lord, this doesn't feel good. I don't know what I'm doing anymore. I can't explain this heaviness, but I have no peace. I'm tired. I'm not sure how I got to this point, but all I can say is forgive me for being the boss of me, for allowing my identity to be wrapped up in my career and caring more about what people have to say about me than what You say about me. I've hurt a lot of people, and I'm tarnishing my image in the process. Please forgive me for my pride and arrogance. I don't want to be the ruler of me anymore, and I don't want to try to figure this out anymore. Open the eyes of my heart. Give me understanding and a softened heart. In Jesus's name, I pray. Amen."

This prayer felt different from the times I'd joined in with the congregation's prayers at church or uttered "God, help me." It was as though I felt the Holy Spirit wrapping Himself around me. Self was the common denominator in all the issues I was facing. Yes, there were folks who had done me wrong, circumstances I was a part of that weren't my fault, but I was allowing it to spill out into other avenues of my life, and that was my fault. I was learning a new way but not applying what I learned to become a new person because I kept choosing to be a victim of my life and choosing outlets I secretly knew wouldn't yield positive results in the search for instant gratification.

The night before, I was at the club trying to fit in with my friends until three a.m. I felt I was in a weird place spiritually and emotionally, like I didn't belong in those types of settings anymore. I was out of place. Internally, I had gotten to a place where I had to make a conscious decision, and God wasn't going to let up on me until I gave in. I gave up. I surrendered all. After I prayed, I just lay there crying more on my bedroom floor, and I felt the heaviness lifted from me. At the age of twenty-four, after being the boss of my life and trying to navigate my pain, my image, my narrative, I decided to let the one who knew His plans for me when He'd formed me in my mother's womb take control.

I was good externally. I was smart. I was handling my business and getting the accolades and support. People loved me, and I was a go-getter. But who was Tiffany at the center, outside of my occupation, achievements, finances, and education? If I pushed all that to the side, what was my drive? Outside of that, I didn't have one. My foundation was built on hiding that broken little girl who kept replaying the trauma of her dad beating her mom and longing for acceptance and trying to prove her worth to people who didn't take the time to notice her. I was the broken little girl who just wished her mother would hug her and let her know she wasn't forgotten.

Once I got off the floor to compose myself, I got into the shower. As I stood in the shower still crying, I knew I needed to rebuild my foundation to heal that broken girl. I got out and turned on Pandora radio. "Wrap Me in Your Arms" by William McDowell played, and all I could hear was a snippet of a scripture in the stillness of the moment in my mind. "Daughter, I have loved you with an everlasting love."

I sat on the couch looking out at my patio, being still. There was such a peace to that moment, like everything would be okay. My email notification chimed on my phone. It was an email from a secretary of a church I had visited while in college inviting me to a two-day seminar called Healthy You, Healthy Me, Heavenly Family. They were serving breakfast and dinner and giving a twenty-five-dollar gift card for completing the training.

What are the chances of me getting this email? I thought. Nothing occurred by happenstance. I clicked the attachments to view more information. The seminar planned to cover a wide range of topics, from effective communication and problem solving, change management, getting to the root of family backgrounds, and identifying healthy relationships.

Wow! I wanted to go, but I felt that I needed someone to go with me. I forwarded the email to my godsister and asked her to attend this two-day event with me. I knew she probably couldn't make the Friday session, but I was open to her coming with me that Saturday. She responded immediately and told me she couldn't make it.

Do I keep searching for someone to go with me, or do I just muster up the courage to go alone? I sent one more email out and didn't get a response. This could've been the moment I'd been waiting for to break free, and I wasn't going to chance it by waiting on a friend to go with me.

I responded to the church secretary and told her to count me in.

Friday came, and I drove to the church after work. Every feeling inside wanted me to go home. I felt sleepy. I wanted to go to the movies. Everything was pointing me in the opposite direction.

As much as I wanted to detour, I drove up to the church. I sat in the car and people watched. I didn't see anyone who was my age walking through those doors. Self-talk told me, *Tiff, just go home now; you're going to stand out.* I didn't know what the next steps behind those doors had for me, but I knew I didn't get that email by mistake, so I owed it to myself to explore further.

I got out of the car and proceeded to walk into the church with every knot imaginable twisting inside my stomach. I signed in and saw my hand shaking just from writing my name. The conference began shortly after I signed in, which I appreciated because I didn't have to converse. As I pulled out my pen and notebook, Napoleon Harrington started it off by jumping right into the heavy topics.

"Relationships are vital—dating, marriage, and friendships—because it's not just a connection between two people; it symbolizes a commitment, a partnership, work that has to be maintained, an understanding of each other's needs. It's a state of connectedness between people. You must determine what your role is in any relationship, if you're a builder or destroyer. Are you excusing your shortcomings and saying you're not responsible? Do you seek to attract attention with an 'It's all about me' mentality? Are you all about gaining power by controlling through manipulation? And do you seek vengeance? These are the key things that destroy relationships. But what builds relationships? Being responsible by thinking before you act and being accountable for your actions; being a contributor not just tangible, but intangible; cooperating by working together and encouraging."

Out of all the relationships I'd had, dating and friendships, I never really defined what a relationship was or identified what made relationships successful. I defined relationships by what I witnessed my parents do, what movies appealed to me, or what I saw on television, but I never put clear intention into truly defining the parameters of success, applying principles like these to the basis of what it should look like.

I was guilty of destroying both types of relationships. Those principles and the role I had played flashed into my mind.

"Some of these might come as a shock. You may have never been taught these in your life," Napoleon said.

Uh, yeah! I thought.

"The thing is, you can fix it. That's why you're here. How? By not criticizing and encouraging alternate behaviors. Give yourself patience and avoid self-discouragement. Use options and not demands. Take the higher road and know your triggers. This avoids many conflicts in relationships. Demands shut the doors to effective communication. If you're angry, find a calmer time for discussions. Understand people's intentions. What's the intention behind the action? Respond to hurt with kindness, and communicate honestly."

The rules seemed easy and clear cut but intimidating and unobtainable. I thought of scenarios I could apply them to, but it felt easier said than done. It seemed with each thought of doubt I had, Napoleon followed up with the next step in the blueprint for success.

"You have to begin with the end in mind. Know what you're getting into before you start relationships. Also, know what you want and don't want. Arguments awaken reason and when done in a healthy way, they aren't bad. In a dating relationship and marriage, it's important that a spiritual connection is established along with a connection to self. If there's no spiritual connection, no relationship to God, no relationship to self, there will be rough roads ahead. If you can beat the feeling game, you will be successful at everything."

Napoleon made me realize that thinking a man was a Christian just because he'd said it and thinking I could fix him or get him into church later was wrong. The reality was I couldn't. He needed to have that for himself. I needed to be solid in this myself before even trying to lead him anywhere.

"Most men and women view God based on their relationship with their dads."

What! My eyes stretched wide open.

I raised my hand. "I'm sorry, can you repeat what you just said? I'm not sure I comprehend the comparison."

"Sure, most men and women view God based on their relationship with their dads. What I mean by that is there is an extreme difference in what we expect and what we get. When you don't get what you want, you have an experience. If our dads are modeled in the likeliness of God and they fail us, we feel God has failed us, too. We go back into the sandbox mentality because of childhood experiences. Most of the conflicts we deal with now are a result of our struggles. You revert to childhood woes, and you don't think clearly because everything is filtered through the lens of hurt. I'm going to leave this here for today. We will pick up on this and more tomorrow."

Tomorrow? There's more? What else is there to go through? I felt like we needed to sit and stew some more on those principles alone. I had questions.

As anxious as I felt when I entered, I left feeling empowered and invested into this seminar. I was glad I came. I was glad I didn't allow the distractions to deter me.

"Thank you, Lord!" That was all I could say as I drove home. I was eager to get home and get some sleep so I could get back first thing in the morning. I giggled as I got into bed, thinking of how when I finally allowed myself to lose control a couple of weeks prior, God sent the resources I needed to heal.

The next day, I purposely arrived with enough time to grab a muffin and juice without having to mingle. As an introvert, I always planned strategic people-avoiding tactics when I ventured anywhere alone. I wasn't there on a social call; I was ready to dive back into more principles but, most importantly, the God and earthly dad comparison.

Napoleon's counterpart instructed the group. "We're going to start the day with breakout sessions to discuss the principles we discussed yesterday. You won't have to move far; you're grouped with your current table."

I let the other people at the table take lead and talk about their thoughts first before I chimed in. Most of the people at my table were married and shared their experiences. I sat and listened until one lady pulled me off the sidelines.

"Honey, you're quiet. What are your thoughts from yesterday?"

"Umm, just processing. These are all new principles that I'm hearing for the first time. I've mainly learned that I've been managing my life all wrong, and I've been horrible to those most connected to me."

Their faces went from smiling and nodding to bleak and emotionless like they weren't ready for my level of honesty.

"Well, okay, thanks for sharing," the woman said.

She gave me a look of distaste, probably because I didn't give a response of hope and positivity, but my response was truthful. I felt my irritation rise. Something on the inside was telling me to leave now. These people didn't want to hear truthful responses.

Napoleon asked, "All right, anyone want to share their table's or personal learnings?"

As irritated as I was by the woman's dismissal of my comment, I fought off the urge to get up and leave and raised my hand.

"Yes, state your name, your church name if you're not a member here, and your learnings."

"My name is Tiffany, Evangel Ministries, and the learning that stuck out for me was that I've been a destroyer of relationships. Though I was brought up in the church, these principles are the first time I'm hearing how my actions impact others in this type of way. But I have a question ..."

"Go ahead."

"You talked about our dads being modeled in the likeliness of God, and when they fail us, we feel God has failed us, too. We go back into the sandbox mentality because of childhood experiences. Most of the conflicts we deal with now are a result of our struggles. Well, my dad is a preacher and abused my mother frequently, and on Sundays, he got up and preached 'thus sayeth the Lord' while some of the churches we attended covered it up. This led to a horrific childhood with caregivers inflicting pain on me, the child, so the destructive principles you talked about, I've personified. Destroy or be destroyed. What do you do when the abuser is rooted in the church, and you know the Word, and you've seen the faithfulness of God, but you keep getting to this stuck point, and you're not sure how to press forward? Because, at the end of the day, my dad is still a 'messenger' of Christ."

The room gasped as I shared, and when I finished, they were silent like a class taking a final exam. Some faces were frozen while others gave me a grimace of dissatisfaction, but not the seminar facilitators.

Napoleon stepped up with a smile. "Tiffany, I appreciate your courage to share. Domestic violence is an epidemic that isn't talked about a lot and has a lot of ramifications that no one is talking about, especially as it pertains to the kids. It takes a lot of intentionality to heal. You must address the trauma through counseling as step one. Any church that condones that is not a church truly following the Bible. Marriage is to reflect

Christ's love for the church. Nowhere do you see Christ abusing the church; therefore, those traits should not be displayed in marriage. Thank you again, Tiffany, I'd like to discuss more with you."

As I took my seat, the facilitators decided to go into day two of the seminar focus, since my question went down a path that obviously others in the room weren't comfortable with. I smiled. Someone valued what I was saying. I'd disrupted the flow in a good way, and I brought awareness into a space that obviously wasn't used to discussing these things.

"We've given you a lot already, but the key thing you must take away is consistency. Consistency is key in all of these principles," Napoleon said.

One thing I hadn't applied to my personal life was consistency, especially in my walk with Christ and dating relationships. I was most consistent with work because that's where I got the most joy and felt accomplished, and they paid me well, so that was easy. The other areas of my soul needed growth in this area. Like water to a plant, consistency was needed to water my soul in the principles of development.

Napoleon interrupted my thoughts with his next statement. "Airplanes with a lot of baggage can't fly. It's up to you to take your health into your own hands as it pertains to your mind, soul, and body. What bags do you need to take off your plane?"

I felt pretty good about dropping off the biggest suitcase weighing down my plane, which was my past relationships. I needed to work on the inward elements, though. A lot of the baggage I was now carrying was internal. Overall, it was a good seminar, and it covered a lot of things I never learned.

As soon as we wrapped and I was preparing to leave, Napoleon stopped at my table. "Tiffany, right?"

"Yes."

"Do you have a moment to chat?"

"Yeah, sure." *Uh oh. Maybe my disruption wasn't that cool,* I thought.

Before he said anything, I jumped right in. "I think I need counseling."

He chuckled. "Okay, what makes you say that? Do you say that because you think that's what I'm going to say to you or because I'm a counselor?"

"Not at all. These past two days, I've learned more about me than I ever have. It provided me insight into why I do a lot of what I do. You heard my background. I've grown up being taught the Bible and in the church, but I'm in this weird space. I'm learning more about the Bible on my own and establishing a relationship with Christ for myself, but I feel like it's not enough. Somehow, in my pursuit to press forward, I keep having these slip ups, and I go back to the past, which keeps tripping me up. So ... Hi, I need counseling."

He laughed and nodded. "You know, I've never had someone, point blank, put it like that, but, yes, counseling is definitely the next step and a big step that you've even acknowledged. I was honestly going to commend you on being so brave and saying what you said in this type of setting."

We exchanged numbers, and I booked my first appointment.

"I've written on my life. It was the final paper in my college journey that's kind of forming into a book if I keep at it. I can send it to you so you have background."

"No, no, the first session is more like an intake where I'll ask guided questions. We'll definitely get to that, though."

"Okay, cool."

17

Sign Me Up

I DIDN'T RAISE MY hand for counseling for the applause or validation from other people; I raised my hand for myself, to show myself that I was committed to the process. I was tired of the back and forth. I wanted to change those negative behaviors versus just taking a plethora of notes with no application. I knew the Bible and all the church clichés, but I didn't know how to apply them practically without getting hung up on people's imperfections, especially my dad.

Counseling was, naturally, my next step. It was a godsend to receive an email alerting me to that conference after praying my prayer of surrender. Yet, growing up, I heard people say only crazy people needed counseling. My dad's famous line was, "I talk to Jesus and friends for free, and can't no counselor tell me nothing." Yet transformation required sacrifice, not just time and money; it was a sacrifice of self.

I decided to sacrifice the hurts, trauma, and past issues. I went through preparation to make myself vulnerable enough to talk to Napoleon about my life before the first appointment after rescheduling many times because of fear. I didn't know what this could look like, and I worried that he wouldn't see my side. After six reschedules, I finally gave in.

I would never know who I could be or who I was made to be when God said He formed me in His image if I didn't take steps to resolve the past pain. I made a list of what I was willing to sacrifice for counseling.

- Sacrifice being hard for being vulnerable
- Sacrifice being on your island of self and submit to the process
- Sacrifice being inconsistent to be consistent and make a concentrated effort to come week after week
- Sacrifice being offended to accept hard truths
- Sacrifice comfort to take ownership
- Sacrifice shrinking to let God stand up in me

Though this list may seem small, for me, it was perfect, but I knew these thematic areas were my weak points. I needed to acknowledge, address, and keep them in front of me at all times so I could tackle them.

I arrived at Napoleon's office scared out of my mind. I pictured the gray couch I always saw on television, me lying out, sharing my life while the counselor took notes, giving minimum feedback, then I'd get to go home.

However, after initial greetings, Napoleon jumped right in. "For our first session, I want you to assess you. Have you done this before?"

"Umm ... I know me, if that's what you're asking. I'm a successful career woman. I've been inducted into the CEO Circle of Excellence—"

"I'm going to stop you and ask you this; how do you assess your feelings or emotions? When you look in the mirror, what truths are you telling yourself? How honest have you been with you?"

"I know my issues, if that's what you're asking, but assessing my feelings … I was never taught to assess my feelings or emotions accurately."

"This is a critical first step. As you grow through life, without this guidance, you will only continue to suppress them, but they'll show up in other ways, which also makes it harder to get to the root of the problem because, now, you have more and more stuff piled on top of it. The first piece of your journey will be for you to begin assessing yourself daily."

As I left, I pondered on what assessing myself daily looked like.

The days following counseling, I got what I called "spirit downloads," which happened when things dropped into my spirit that I wasn't thinking about, yet they aligned with what I was doing. I'd review and ponder over my counseling notes when suddenly, I'd get one of those spirit downloads.

I heard, *List your priorities,* so I grabbed a notebook and listed what I felt was important to me at the time.

1. Daily prayer and devotional/reading my Word
2. Going to work
3. Making sure the key elements of my job are done
4. Making sure the key elements of church work is done

This list was eye-opening because it was two dimensional with most of the focus on work—clearly off balance. On another day, I heard, *List what you're thinking about all the time,* which revealed that I'm a tad bit scatterbrained. Who am I kidding? I'm *very* scatterbrained. But I realized the thoughts that consistently floated through my mind were task oriented, financial decisions, negative assessments of people, and ways to shape my future.

From there, I began getting into a rhythm. As my spirit led, I wrote: *List where you go all the time, who you consistently talk to, what you're watching on TV, what you're eating, the phrases that consistently come out of your mouth, the sites you go to on the Internet.*

Upon returning for my second session, I had a ton of notes to share and was excited about the progress we'd made from the first week of doing the work. Daily assessments started my journey. It was a much more involved session than I originally thought it would be as Napoleon's strategy was based on ensuring I had the tools for application.

However, if the assessment wasn't enough, Napoleon went on to tell me that in addition to assessing myself, which was an ongoing work, he wanted me to analyze the relationships in my life along with every thought, feeling, and trigger.

"My goal is to make you dig up the pain of the past to address it. Assessment, analysis, and seeking to understand is hard work, but it's worth it. A lot of the behaviors in your assessment, I can tell you, has a reaction connected to it that's based on experiences of your past, when you were younger, and we're going to get to the root. I want to do a mind map activity with you to visually display who's connected to you. Each bubble is a representation of who is connected to you. We're going to talk out each relationship and the attributing feelings— good, bad, and indifferent—to measure if your assessment of the relationship is factual or myth."

I felt my attitude rise in my spirit. *Myth? Everything I said is facts! How is he going to challenge my assessment? It's my assessment, so of course it's factual!*

However, as we went through the mind mapping activity, my irritation shifted to tears. It identified deeper feelings that needed to be explored more, which was just the baseline. I had doubted his methods, but it proved that only half my assessment was factual.

"Once you visually see how each bubble affects you and the emotions connected, there's no way one person can carry all this emotional baggage."

It showed me the people I needed in my life as key supporters and aides in my transition and growth and those who shouldn't be connected to me.

"The ones we've identified as those who should be connected to you are your trusted voices. Allow them to give their honest feedback about what they observe about you. If you don't have friends who can tell you the truth and only tell you what you want to hear or the fun stuff, you will never grow; you're still on an island of self. They're able to see your blind spots, the areas you can't. It will be uncomfortable at first because it requires you to allow others in your space, which ultimately requires you to be vulnerable."

I internally cringed. I always wore the mask as the strong one, the one who could take on the world, who had all the answers and could get it done. When I reflected, I realized I only allowed two or three people to tell me the truth about myself. My current circle was about having a good time.

"As you heal, also be on the lookout for the next phase of people God will send your way. They will be sent to help you solidify the next step of the vision for your life, but it starts with the understanding that not all people who tell you the truth about yourself are your enemies."

I inherited that trait from my dad. Anyone who dared tell him the truth about himself was his enemy, and subconsciously, I fell into the same habit. I was always offended before I took the time to process if what they were saying was helpful or hurtful. Based on this activity, there were certain friends I needed to let go. Everyone couldn't go with me, and those were the ones who enabled me to function in my dysfunction.

Even though I was having great sessions with Napoleon, I wanted to stop counseling several times. Every session got harder and harder. I rescheduled a lot because I didn't like how I felt when leaving some of the sessions. In the beginning, I shed a lot of tears as we gutted my issues. If I had a hard day at work, I intentionally rescheduled my appointment because I didn't want to deal with the emotions afterward, or if I didn't apply the tools I'd been learning from him and my sermons and resorted back to my defaults, I'd feel an enormous amount of shame and guilt.

Counseling revealed to me that I was comfortable walking around hurt and it was easy to hold on to the hurt and anger in an effort to protect myself, but the longer I held onto those things, the more I kept infecting my mind, body, and soul and couldn't grow into the new Tiffany I was destined to be. Therefore, no matter how much of a struggle it was and how many times I'd purposely missed our appointment and rescheduled, I still kept myself accountable to the process. I sent Napoleon email updates, so he still stayed in the know and knew I was still committed to the process, even though I had been ducking our face-to-face sessions. Some emails were angrier than others, and when I'd go to my next session, he'd meet me right at that email.

"I read your email, and wow! Tell me what happened."

I shared with him my recap and how certain events made me feel.

He jumped in. "You notice as you tell this story, your voice inflection goes up? You're forcing your point."

"No, I'm passionate about it."

"When you're reacting with those voice inflections, it feels as though you're defensive and forcing your point. No one can hear you when you react like that. It's natural you do that because you come from a home that communicated in anger at every turn. However, the calmer you are, the more insight you're able to clearly articulate with your point while also providing solutions, which will allow you to win a whole lot more battles."

It made a lot of sense.

"When words hurt you, you default to nine-year-old Tiffany. Let's talk triggers. You have very distinct trigger points."

"I do?"

"Yes, and they're based on what you're doing in the moment, who you're experiencing in that moment, and the type of spirit they remind you of, whether it be your dad or someone of your past. One of the biggest triggers I see for you is expectations."

I had no response because everything he was saying was true.

"When your expectations aren't being met, you default to operating out of hurt like nine-year-old Tiffany by saying and doing things that don't always reflect your heart. You must learn to separate your words from your heart. When wounded, your heart and words become defensive. When anger is your friend, it hardens your heart against people, which goes against what the Bible says: 'Love God and love people. You can't love God and not like His people' (1 John). You also don't have to respond to everything. When you're confident about where you are and the Christ in you, no one can shake that foundation. As you develop in this area, expect irritations but begin working harder on not letting them take you out of your center."

I put my pen and notebook down and stared off into space. I was ready to end the session.

Napoleon was great with discerning how much I could handle in our sessions. "We've discussed a lot. Take some time and marinate on everything I've said and your notes. See you next week?"

"I suppose."

During every session, my decisions were based on Winston Churchill's statement: "Am I going to stand up and speak or sit down and listen?"

18

The Personification
of Purpose

WHILE LEAVING A COUNSELING session one evening, I received a call from my goddad.

"Hello, daughter."

"Hey, Dad."

"You've been showing great potential and doing a great job. I want you to assist me with running the worship and media department."

I laughed. "Well, first off ... Aww, thanks. Secondly, what's the responsibilities, and I have to ask why. I'd have to interact more with the senior leadership of the church. Pastor Brooks is going to have an issue with that."

"I'll handle that; remember, I told you you're protected. Your reputation is redeeming itself with the work you do. You proved to be trustworthy and responsible as well as very smart. You have a hunger for worship and music, and you're a techie like your dad. I believe the Lord has touched you and given you a special gifting when it comes to understanding the heart of worship. In discovering your skillset, this is a perfect next step for you to build our relationship and the department. You'll be handling everything from the front office and pastoral communications, requests, scheduling, managing the budget, team leader alignment, meeting management, process creation and refinement, and you'll be the floor director for the annual fall concert."

"I appreciate that, but I'm still not confident. This is more visibility, more people interaction, and I'm still not the best with people, so maybe you shouldn't be putting me in this role."

"Daughter, what you experienced and witnessed while being raised sums up who you were when you acted out. Since you've been my daughter, we've discovered that you must separate that experience and create a new mindset and atmosphere based on your Heavenly Dad's love by sitting in the presence of the Lord. It takes time to shed the hardness and the sharp edges. You've been given this opportunity to be you and make a choice to transform into a better person in Christ. Trust is important to me, and I wanted to build trust with you so you can begin to trust again. With much that is given, much is required. You've earned it."

"Hmm ... I hear you. But what are you seeing that I can't see in all this? I want to accept, but I don't want to fail."

"I understand that, but you won't. I have great faith in you, daughter."

I wasn't used to being celebrated, being affirmed, or people having faith in me, so it was hard to accept.

Pastor Bonner wasn't playing any games. My first and biggest project was being floor director for a special fall concert with our choir and dance team. I was responsible for coordinating and booking rehearsal space, budget alignment, visual illustrations, graphic and invitation creation, timeline management, and program flow. As I handled my tasks, a song the choir was practicing by Torrance Greene called "He Knows My Name" caught my heart.

From the time the band kicked it off until the choir joined

in with the lyrics, it felt like a love song from God to me. That song met me right where I was spirituality, emotionally, and mentally. Counseling and being connected to the right church that was teaching sound biblical principles created a safe space for me and aided in my transformation.

After my blow out with the youth director, I had insecurities that told me the other leaders of the church wouldn't listen, support me, or respect me, and I'd have to, once again, prove who I was and wasn't for acceptance, but I was constantly challenged by Pastor Bonner to put the guard down. Pastor Brooks reminded me that "everything we do is based as unto the Lord" (1 Corinthians 10:31), and scripture made me stop proving myself and come with a heart of servitude. My heart to serve God's people, be humble, and be creative showed up. My gifts made room for me. Serving in ministry, I gained more insight into my passions and connected them to my spiritual gifts more and more.

Pastor Bonner taught me to pay more attention to the hearts of people, not just completing the task. Starting off, I was task driven, but I began to connect more with people through serving. Serving was more fulfilling than going to work every day. To be able to see how my actions weren't just impacting me, but others' lives and seeing life change as the fruit.

I was in awe that God would use me in such a way, especially with the missteps I'd taken along the way. God continued to show Himself as the redeemer.

I received a special email from Pastor Brooks:

> *Hey Tiff – I'm very happy to announce that the leaders and clergy have been so impressed with your contribution to our church this year that they selected you to be our 2010 Volunteer of the Year. We will be recognizing you during our New Year's Eve service. Thanks for being such an awesome role model.*

I was overcome with excitement and shock. *Volunteer of the Year?* My mind was blown. On top of receiving the award, Pastor Brooks allowed Pastor Bonner to give me my award. His speech before calling me up to get my award left me speechless.

"Diamonds are made from compressed coal that is under pressure for long periods of time and must be dug out of the deep mines in the earth. Diamonds don't just lay around the ground all sparkly and brilliant. You must dig deep to find them. You then must examine them after much pressure cleaning and apply friction and cutting to bring out the color and brilliance that shows its true value. I saw you and see you, daughter. Although you have come through a very revealing and important season of your life, there is still much to learn in your continued transformation. I am glad you allowed me to be a small part of that, daughter, and appreciate all you've brought to these departments, our church, and the Kingdom."

I cried. That award hit differently for me from all the awards I'd received in my life. It showed me that though I had a hard time comprehending, God affirmed me. He marked me, and it all had purpose. The ministry I'd tried to outrun and distance myself from was what saved me from me.

Full-time work and full-time ministry left me busy, and Napoleon offered me no slack. He didn't take his foot off the gas at all.

"When's the last time you processed your feelings and marinated in the moment?"

I couldn't answer. "I don't know."

"For someone with the workload you have, that's normal, but you need to go back to the beginning and process your feelings. This time, you, most importantly, need to hear your thoughts and appreciate the stillness of moments."

"Hear my thoughts?"

"You have so much noise, whether it's family, work, or

church, you can't enjoy the moment. Hear yourself or hear clear thoughts. When's the last time you were in peace and quiet?"

"Umm ... I don't know."

"Practice peace. Embrace quiet moments. Turn your mind off. A lot of noise keeps you from feeling your feelings, and the noise keeps you from feeling you. You probably aren't aware of this, but when growing up in a home like yours, it's not unnormal to keep yourself busy to quiet the trauma in your mind and heart. Those practices and habits just follow you as you go through life. To escape your feelings, you stay working by giving yourself success goals, which ultimately works against you because you're working yourself to exhaustion, and that's very unhealthy."

He made a good and valid point, but I quickly interjected. "But Napoleon, a big part of my personality is my drive. My drive fuels me. I'm just naturally wired this way."

"Yeah, but it also gives you escape syndrome, which pushes you into overdrive, where you have to feel needed to do over and beyond. You have to allow your mind to rest and not fill it up with busyness every waking moment."

What could I say to that?

Napoleon gave me activities to implement to practice quieting my mind.

At work, I was promoted from the IT department to the marketing department with no experience and was gifted another amazing boss, Barry. Barry worked to develop me, put me on the road, and got me connected with an amazing mentor. He also gave me the creative freedom to follow my gut instinct to test ideas, implement processes, and give input. He gave me a seat at the table countless times to ensure I received visibility.

God began setting up big things and situations for me, so I'd have to undeniably say, *God did this*. I'm not the best to ever do it. There are wiser, smarter people who are more deserving than me. I didn't do everything the right way, but God kept putting me in these positions. I trusted God, and He kept moving on my behalf. The scriptures I kept reading were no longer words on a page, I was watching them come to life.

All this time, I was trying to be what culture dictated I should be when just being who God created me to be was opening opportunities far beyond anything I could have put together on my own. This new level of elevation required me to completely trust in God. I couldn't walk around with my chest puffed out like I did when I first started the job because of who I was transforming into. I was allowing pride to be my identity, which wasn't leaving room for God to take me where I needed to go.

He renewed my sense of trust and gave me a greater confidence, and as my confidence grew, I gave Him greater credit. Being in the new department introduced me to traveling, which I was open to. I always wanted to travel for work with no restrictions before I got married and had a family. When I got married, I didn't want to split my time with work travel instead of being at home with my husband and children, so while I was single, I was ready to live it up. I continued to pursue Christ aggressively while serving full-time in the Worship and Media Ministry, traveling the U.S. and getting counseling.

There were things on which I had constructed my life, not conscious of my identity in Christ and what I possessed on the inside. As I evolved and healed, my identity no longer agreed with being established from present situations. I wasn't content with my identity being rooted in my past issues, people's opinions, or on my career anymore. It was now being shaped in Christ, and I was seeing the fruits of that. Like fruit of an orchard, so was the fruit of love, a genuine affection for others, a newly formed exuberance about life as I traveled more and had new experiences. Most importantly, serenity blossomed. I began developing a willingness to stick with things versus being quick to cut people off. I did cut off the wrong people, but I developed a patience for those who had the right intentions but were just having a bad day. I used to cut everyone off, but Napoleon was instrumental in teaching me the difference.

The fruits of counseling and living out the Bible as my roadmap along with being intentional were highly visible to those closest to me and those who hadn't connected with me yet. Those closest to me wanted to be around me more. Prior to counseling and rededicating my life to Christ, I walked around hurting, not knowing I was hurt, yet masking it as "showing them" while I self-destructed. I had been internally bleeding for a long time before it began to spill out onto others. One of the first things I did upon my life change was intentionality seek restoration with those I had split out on.

Even those I previously offended could see the new Tiffany. They didn't have to be afraid that I would cut them with my words or be hypersensitive and take everything they said as an attack. Once I saw there were people in my life who were meant to sharpen me, I kept them close and held tight. God used those people of influence to get me to the next level, and it helped me get where I needed to go. Life was finally turning the tide for me and heading in a direction far beyond anything I could have imagined.

19

Here We Go Again

ON MY JOURNEY TO transformation, I shockingly entered another relationship. It was a slow start. Cordell was a friend of Tyler's. We connected through Facebook, commenting on statuses here and there until we exchanged numbers. Our friendship began just as Damien and I were ending our relationship, and I would share with him what was going on. Cordell knew I wasn't ready for a relationship because my ex had taken a chunk from me mentally, emotionally, and financially. To my surprise, Cordell had a similar situation, and he was living with his girlfriend, but explained that his relationship was going south, and they were only roommates. Although I was able to quickly pivot and get out of my living arrangement, Cordell was not. I excused it because I was in that predicament before, and with financial commitments, it wasn't always easy to detach.

He lived in North Carolina and had a great career, good values, and he was financially stable, which was light years ahead of any of the guys I'd dated thus far. The most intriguing thing we had in common was that both our dads were Baptist preachers. I didn't force him to match my spiritual walk, especially after the Healthy Conference I attended. I wanted to see where he was spiritually for myself, and even though I didn't interfere, I was quite vocal about where I was with growing in my relationship with Christ and serving my local church. He served in his local church, too, which was also more than the guys I previously dated had done. We could talk about any and everything, from office politics, television shows, and movies, but his favorite hobbies were riding his motorcycle and video games.

My mom moved to North Carolina with Tyler in early 2010 to see if she liked the change of environment. While there, she gave me an interesting call.

"Hello, daughter," she said.

"Hey, Ma."

"How's everything going?"

"Fine. What's up? I'm just getting in from work and need a nap bad."

"Well, there is this guy here who I feel would be perfect for you."

"Oh, yeah ..."

I wasn't interested. My mom tried to play matchmaker in late 2007 with a "church boy," and it was a disastrous attempt that pushed me back into Derek's arms. I probably would've ended it sooner with Derek had that atrocious attempt at matchmaking not happened. I didn't want her suggestions.

"Yes, girl. He's so respectful and very nice. I could totally see you two together."

"Mom, no thanks. I'm on the road to inner healing and wholeness, and I don't have time."

"You should really give him a chance. For him to be Tyler's friend, I like him a lot for you."

Tyler's friend? I was curious now. Could it be?

"Tyler's friend, who?"

"Cordell!"

I chuckled.

"What's so funny?"

"I know Cordell. We're already friends."

"Well, you need to date him, girl."

"Umm, not interested, Mother, and he already has a girlfriend."

"Oh, girl, you got her beat, and they don't seem like they're together like that."

"Appreciate you, but I'm good. We gone keep it as is. Talk to you later!"

I smiled as I settled myself for the evening because it was cute and affirming that my mom approved of him. A couple of months went past, and he began pursuing me with my mom as his biggest supporter. I stood strong and even threw darts his way, showing the unfavorable side of me by not returning calls, being attitudinal, and giving unasked for, overly critical opinions during his decision making. He remained unfazed. I shared with him secrets of my past to deter him, and, still, he didn't budge. While on a road trip with my godfamily, he was so caring and attentive and wanted every detail to ensure my safety.

I decided, *Okay, let's see where this is going.* That was always what I craved in my relationships, to feel and be protected. I booked a flight to visit him, and he exceeded all my expectations. From opening car doors, to motorcycle rides, paying for all the activities (I tried to pay for myself, but he wouldn't allow it), and dropping me off at the hotel without trying to convince me of why he should stay the night. He was a true southern gentleman.

The only red flag—his girlfriend—was no longer a factor because, supposedly, at the top of 2011, they ended their relationship and were only roommates. In the back of my mind, I compared my relationship with Robin (and her main girlfriend) to Cordell and his ex to see if there were any similarities, and there weren't any on the surface. Cordell seemed to be a natural fit for me. He'd seen the good and bad sides of me and only wanted to know and encourage me more. I thought, *I can handle this.*

He flew out to visit me next, and within four hours of his arrival, I got food poisoning. As I battled diarrhea and non-stop vomiting over the toilet, he held my hair and passed me the trashcan. He escorted me back to the bed and gave me washrags to clean up. He also made store runs to get medicine for me. For taking care of me in that critical state, I deemed him my future husband and moved full steam ahead. My mother was right.

I took him to meet everyone—my work family, church family, friends, and blood family. There was a half-and-half split in opinions. The half that didn't agree, I thought were haters.

I was in love and on cloud nine when things began to change. Consistency turned into inconsistency quickly. He was part of a bike club, and outside of work, that was his focus. And other things I hadn't noticed began to surface.

Cordell wouldn't stay at the hotel when I came to visit because he had to get back to his apartment so his supposed ex-girlfriend wouldn't think anything was wrong. Initially, I didn't think it was a problem because, as I had already communicated to him, I wasn't having sex until marriage and wasn't sacrificing my purity pledge. However, I was also informed that he was still making appearances with her as a couple, which made me think maybe they *were* still a couple. He prioritized trips with the bike club over visits we could have had and gave snide comments about me always being at church. Cordell mentioned he wasn't fazed by my purity pledge, but as the relationship went on, he wasn't with it and became more forceful when asking.

"What you compromise to keep, you'll eventually lose" floated in my thoughts. I didn't want to compromise on my pledge. With the pressure of distance and not wanting him to cheat, I sent him pictures, but the red flags popped up again, that gut feeling that told me although he was a great guy, I didn't feel he was the one

for me. The one for me would understand, stay consistent, and respect my pledge to purity and Christ.

Over the span of four years, our relationship was a rollercoaster ride. It was the longest relationship I'd been in, and the love I had for him exceeded what I had with even my high school boyfriend. A lot of our arguments were based on my growth into womanhood. As I continued my evolution with counseling, studying the Bible, and being consistent with the principles I learned, I understood what I wanted and didn't want but, most importantly, what and who God wanted for me, and it was different based on the circumstance. I was learning as I went along, discovering my new identity and pursuing healing. I thought I could juggle healing, spiritual growth, a career, and a new relationship, but I couldn't.

I thought I could handle him still living with his supposed ex-girlfriend, but I couldn't. The unresolved issues with my past relationships were showing up all over the place. I told myself it was okay, that I was secure, and he was upfront, but as time revealed itself, that wasn't the case. Too many opinions were added into the mix, from my goddad to Cordell's best friend. Multiple people told me, "He's not the one for you."

I denied it, but the signs kept following. He was cool with me being in church if I didn't try to force my level of commitment on him. Spiritually, we saw things differently and, again, I was trying to make him see things from my lens, but that wasn't my place. We discussed marriage many times, but our spirituality differences were a big issue. I was more traditional in what I wanted, and I wasn't compromising. This became a problem because, though we were very ambitious with our careers and climbing corporate ladders, I was willing to drop my career for the sake of marriage and family. He didn't want that.

In the pursuit of careers and corporate climbs, we argued a lot. Though we could talk about any and everything, we couldn't resolve problems effectively. We also didn't communicate the same. Despite all these red flags, along with the knowledge I'd gained from my past failed relationships, I didn't want to admit that I was in another bad relationship. So, though unhappy, I kept overlooking it.

In my heart, I felt we were always supposed to be friends, and the purpose of our friendship was to lead him closer to Christ. I learned that not everyone was supposed to be my man. I had other guy friends whom I'd consistently kept in the friend zone, but for some reason, I kept asking myself why I didn't have the same courage to keep Cordell as a friend.

20

Transformative Shifts

SOME MONTHS PASSED, AND I settled into my new role in marketing. The job required that I travel monthly. In the fall of 2012, my travels led me to a business visit in Phoenix, Arizona. It was my first visit, and I loved it. My mom informed me I had a cousin who lived there whom I hadn't seen since 2002. She's my oldest cousin, and every time I encountered her at a family event, she was nice to me, so I reached out to her to meet up after my business meetings before I flew out.

The drive to her place boasted gorgeous views. At the end of our visit as I walked to the car to head to the airport, I turned to them and said, "This time next year, I'll be living here!"

In the winter of 2013, I wanted a career change and had many mentor meetings and conversations with my boss, Barry. My work travels had me visiting the West Coast a lot. Between California and Arizona, I felt a shift in my spirit that told me it was time to move. In April, Barry called me to his desk to discuss an option. "There's some changes and promotions coming down the pipeline. A field marketing coach position will be opening in North Carolina. Do you think you would be interested?"

I could hardly contain my excitement.

"Yes! Cordell, my mom, and brother live there. I'm familiar with the area. But ... I don't have field marketing experience."

"Let me see what I can do."

Barry had a conversation with the field marketing manager and came back to me.

"We're going to send you to Baltimore to job shadow. You're going to shadow one of the coaches and let us know what you want to do. Book your flight for next week."

It took everything in me not to run back to my desk. I booked my flight quickly, and the trip was great. I loved what I saw and caught on to the role instantly. I even had ideas for improvement, which they loved. I submitted an executive summary to recap my learnings and takeaways to show I was serious about the position.

In May, I was offered the position, but the relocation was to Salt Lake City, not North Carolina. I wasn't as excited as I thought I would be, and Barry could tell.

"I can tell this is a shock. Is it the Salt Lake piece?"

"Mmm ... Yes. I'm grateful, don't get me wrong. Thank you for the offer, but what happened to North Carolina?"

"That's a big market with a lot of challenges, and it wouldn't be fair to send you there to learn while expecting you to turn the market around at the same time."

"Ah, okay."

"Take some time to think it over and let me know."

I talked to God about it before anyone else.

"God, you know I'm not feeling this. If it's in Your will for me to move, this opportunity will come back around, but I'm not feeling it."

I didn't feel peace in my spirit about it. I knew I wanted to move, but I didn't want to just move anywhere for the sake of moving. My inner critic jumped in. *You put yourself out there, now you're going to take it back? That doesn't look good for your career. Shows you're unsure.* As loud as the inner critic was, it didn't change my decision. I shared my thoughts with my family as well as Pastor Brooks and Pastor Bonner as my coverings, and they supported my decision, too.

I respectfully declined. Barry understood and applauded me for not giving in to the pressure. Two weeks later, the day after Memorial Day, he called me and said they wanted to offer me the same position but this time in Phoenix. I would be the field marketing coach over fifty-eight corporate stores. They wanted me to relocate by the beginning of July, but I needed to fly out the following week to job shadow the current coach as she was getting promoted to the North Carolina position. I was overcome with excitement.

As I drove in to work, I could do nothing but scream, cry, and thank God. After my moment of thanksgiving, I called my mom and told her the great news. "You're coming with me," I told her.

My mom had come back home from North Carolina the spring of 2013 to help care for my goddad's mother before she passed away from cancer, and we got a condo together shortly after.

"What do you mean I'm coming?" she asked.

"You heard me; you're coming. Fresh start, and you don't have to worry about what you're going to do when I leave."

She was overcome with joy but terrified as well because she was moving far away from the people she'd known her whole life. Others weren't as excited as I thought they would be and tried to get me to second guess my move. Before counseling, I probably would have listened. However, a year prior and at the top of 2013, I really began hearing the voice of the Lord for myself, so it didn't matter what opinions others had for me or what box they felt I should stay in. I reached a pivotal point and stopped looking back and asking other folks what they thought.

I simply trusted that God's hand was on me and consulted Him more with what He thought I should be doing. It felt good to say I heard from God and made my decision with my newfound God-fidence (confidence in God). All of this came after I surrendered. I had to surrender, let the "stuff" go, and unlearn certain things to learn new things. I decided to surrender and realign my life by doing the work necessary to become healthy and whole.

When I took my eyes off what I wanted and stopped trying to control and manufacture my blessings in every area, God blessed me far beyond what I could see and think. What I didn't foresee was the impact my decision to leave would have on people. The responses to my move were all over the board from various family members and friends.

"Just like that, you're going to just go?"

"You're going to leave your family?"

"You've never been there before; how are you going to just up and leave?"

"What about your nieces and nephews?"

"I've always wanted to move to another state but didn't want to just up and leave like you're doing. So bold!"

None of it deterred me, and I answered with a smile. Old Tiff would've answered with irritation, yet Christ was using me as an example to show the open door of possibilities for people who were considering what God had encouraged and called them to do.

Napoleon told me, "Your move to the desert has to happen. It's symbolic to this new season in your life. It's showing your free-falling trust in God and what happens when you surrender and allow Him to order your steps. Even through the fear, this shows your faith in God is greater than allowing an emotion to control you."

I cried a lot of tears, but I was ready for the new season.

Cordell came in town to celebrate my relocation to Phoenix. The weekend was supposed to be all about me and my going away party. But our vibe was off from the time his plane landed.

I arrived at his hotel as he was still getting ready for church. Upon my arrival, he got into the shower. While I sat and waited, his phone kept going off.

I felt something in the pit of my gut. I knew this feeling, and I felt the anger rising in my chest. He came out of the bathroom half-dressed, and I was pissed off.

"What's wrong?" he asked.

"Oh, nothing. Can I see your phone? I want to put it on Spotify."

He handed over his phone, I opened Spotify then quickly went to his call and text message logs. The feeling in my stomach was confirmed by the messages I read from another woman who had sent pictures and stated how much she missed him. Lines he once said to me, he was now saying to her.

"You want to tell me who this chick is you've been texting?" I asked.

He stood frozen then deflected. "You went through my phone? When we start doing this?"

"It wouldn't matter if you didn't have anything to hide!"

"But you went through my phone, and you lied."

"First off, I didn't lie. See, Spotify is up. Don't try to put this on me. You're trying to deflect, when your phone has been going off nonstop since I've been here. Why did you come here? Why? It's my weekend, and you come here with this?"

"I wanted to celebrate you."

"Celebrate me? Don't celebrate me if this is the type of mess you bring!"

I was angry to the point of tears. I hadn't felt that type of anger and hurt in a long time, and I felt myself gasping for air. I sat on the couch to compose myself.

"I'm sorry. I'll just fly out earlier than my scheduled departure time."

"No! You're going to deal with all this today before your

flight. You're not going to embarrass me and leave now. Hurry up and get dressed."

I stormed out of the hotel room to wait in the car. I hated that I felt I needed him to keep up the image. I wore a mask that showed that I had an awesome career and a supportive man, but the reality was he was bad for me. There was love between us, but it was just a counterfeit of the love I desired, needed, and was meant to have.

He got into the car, and I sped off. We were late for church. As I flew down the freeway, he wanted to have a heart-to-heart that made me more frantic.

"I'm really sorry," he said.

"You're sorry you got caught," I said as I sped in a fury, crossing lanes to scare him and shut him up.

"No, I'm really sorry. I didn't get the job I wanted, and you've been overly busy with this new promotion you got. I needed someone to pay me some attention."

That infuriated me even more. "You have got to be kidding me! So because I get a promotion, and I'm relocating during the most exciting time of my life, you decide to cheat? That makes a *ton* of sense, Cordell."

The car went silent, and I was glad. He needed to hear the echo of his own stupidity.

When we got to church, worship was still going on. They were singing "Called to Be" by Jonathan Nelson.

Worship always got me back to the center of myself. It was where I could be most desperate for God. I poured myself out into the praise and worship, as angry as I was, and began crying out while singing the words to that song. The lyrics of the song were affirmations that I was still going to be who God called me to be regardless of yet another misstep. As worship ended and the praise team was transitioning to the next phase of service, I abruptly walked out without telling Cordell where I was going. I was on my way to my goddad's office to tell him what happened when Cordell jumped up to follow me.

My friend AJ was just coming off stage after singing with the praise team. "Hey, Tiff!" he said, followed by a joke that made me smile. Worship got me out of my funk, and AJ was the icing on the cake.

"Hey, AJ, come to Pastor Bonner's house this evening for my going away party."

"For real?"

"Yes, I want you there. Say you'll come, please."

"For you, I'll be there."

"Okay, cool. Get with Gina; she'll give you the details."

The bond AJ and I shared was so noticeable that Cordell asked, "You sure y'all just friends? Seems like more to me."

"Like I said, he's my friend, but you can't really talk with your current situation," I snapped back.

AJ could've snatched me away from Cordell, but we didn't have that type of relationship. When I first took notice of AJ in choir rehearsal a year prior and considered the possibility of us being more than friends, my goddad said, "Absolutely not."

"Hey, Dad," I had asked. "Who's the new tenor? He's cute, funny, and spiritually sexy. He's in tune with the Bible, isn't ashamed to be sold out for Christ, isn't afraid to tap into praise and worship, and he even cries while he worships God. I've never seen that."

"No, daughter. He just got divorced. He's working on himself and growing spiritually, and you are, too. You both need to focus on your spiritual growth."

So AJ was friend zoned. My goddad didn't approve, and I adhered to that. He was the closest thing to a father in my life since my birth dad wasn't present in this season, so I obeyed.

In the weeks to come, Cordell's apologies for cheating were followed by expensive gifts instead of changed behavior. At first,

I thought it was cute. I forgave him and went along, showing off my new presents.

But when my goddad saw the gifts come in, especially one of the most expensive ones, he said, "Give them back."

"What? Are you crazy? He paid six hundred dollars for this. I deserve this after all he's been putting me through."

It wasn't until later that I remembered that was how my dad apologized to my mom for his abuse. He'd buy her expensive gifts like furs, new cars, clothes, and diamonds. I couldn't keep turning a blind eye and receiving gifts to make the problems disappear.

After years of an off-and-on relationship and allowing a man to perceive me as an option instead of his choice, I finally got to a place where my time nor my healing was waiting for anybody. I needed to choose me above all else, and no gift or amount of money could make me change my mind. The man I was to be with needed to come ready and prepared, and though Cordell had known me for years, he wasn't prepared. Our relationship wasn't enough for what I needed.

My sessions with Napoleon also revealed that while on my journey of healing and wholeness, this relationship showed me I was struggling with independence and vulnerability. I felt if I were independent, I couldn't be vulnerable, and if I was vulnerable, I couldn't be independent.

"Tiffany, pure relationships have both. Vulnerability and independence can be exhibited at the same time with the right man, and your Mr. Right will handle it properly. However, if you are vulnerable and mishandled, it will take you to a bad head space. With the right man, you can afford to have those emotions because it's healthy, but you can't afford to walk through those emotions without the support of the right man to walk you through them."

It was clear that I was manufacturing my relationship again instead of letting God do it. I couldn't afford anymore slip-ups or compromises because the more I grew and became rooted spiritually, the more convicted I became in my spirit. With one wrong decision, all the work I'd done to get to this point would have dwindled, so I decided to be obedient to the Bible. After years of being tossed to and fro, I finally decided to end the relationship, but I knew he hadn't gotten the picture. We had perfected the breakup-to-makeup cycle, but this time, I knew I wasn't interested in sticking around to see if this was the time he'd finally understand.

My counselor helped me define the end without looking back.

"Tiffany, we're going to roll play. I'm him. What are you going to say?"

As I began to share, my counselor threw curveballs into the conversation, portraying Cordell perfectly. He even threw in romantic angles. I stuck to what I was saying. He diverted and tried to blame shift. I almost jumped into defending myself, but I noticed what he was doing, so I stayed on script.

"Good. Everything you just said, write it down, and consider all the different angles he may throw at you. It's okay to be sincere, but be firm. The minute you go off script or your anger appears, everything will be up in the air, and you'll show him he still has a chance. Remain in control, but shut it down with ease. Insert truth filled with grace, yet be forceful. Show him the calmer Tiffany."

It was bittersweet because I'd invested so much time, energy, and emotions. If it was in God's will for me to be married, I'd be married. Until then, I wanted to continue chasing after the things of the Lord and becoming my best self. If the man didn't love the Lord more than me and wasn't dedicated to following the Bible, then we had nothing in common. My counselor's last statement of our session stood out.

"If a man loves the Lord more than you and desires to live

out the Word for his life, then loving you will be easy because he's already in tune with the one who created him to love you."

Relationships became my drug. I longed to feel loved and protected, like I belonged, and I felt the only way to be loved and make up for being forgotten and neglected for so long was to have boyfriends. I knew I didn't want to be abused like my mom, so I tolerated other dysfunctions in its place. I took on other forms of abuse during my failed attempts to control my relationships. Every relationship I had in my life gave me a lesson about myself and, ultimately, pushed me closer to Christ.

When my plane landed in Phoenix, it was official—My season had changed. My new job was challenging, but I tapped into the greater dependence I had in Christ. I was equipped with the tools I learned in the Word, counseling, and my job. However, there were days I had no clue about what to do next or what to propose, and it was in those moments, I stopped, prayed, and worshipped, and God gave me strategy.

I took on a market that hadn't made the company money in years. It was the corporate problem child of the business. The pressure to make an impact was great. I smiled because I knew God was greater. The creativity that flowed through my marketing plans within a few months was God inspired and unlike anything my leaders had seen in that market.

However, with this promotion, I felt alone. Even though my mom moved with me, my closest family and friends were 1,600 miles away. The biggest adjustment was not having a church home. I missed the connection with other church goers who had become family, being in a place of strong worship and solid word. It was one thing to feel alone when I was surrounded by a lot of people, but to be totally moved from the environment where I could just do a pop-up visit to my best friend's house was something I had to adjust to.

I traveled back home bi-quarterly for corporate office

meetings, and it allowed me to see those I missed, but it wasn't the same.

I would travel all over to see friends and family before flying back to Phoenix, and it was exhausting.

Upon returning, these words dropped into my spirit: *He sent you to live in the valley of the sun to get you alone.*

He moved me away because I couldn't afford to be distracted, and I was still distracted. Initially, when I moved to Phoenix, I was still trying to handle family and church business as my goddad's assistant. The epiphany that came after those words was clear—If I kept myself in the same environment, even when I was thousands of miles away, I was still there. I would be on the verge of losing myself by trying to satisfy everyone else's needs. I was mishandling my gift.

In some cases, I wasn't even using my gift. I had to consistently learn and practice what it meant to free myself from other things that would take over my mind and not allow me to complete the mission I was sent to Phoenix for—my job.

I talked to Napoleon about the cognitive dissonance I was experiencing, and he dropped some wisdom on me.

"God wants to build something in you and reveal it while you're there in the desert, but He can't if you won't be present in the moment. Tiffany, it is time for you to be self-interested, not selfish, but interested in self. When flying, the flight attendant instructs the passengers to secure their own oxygen masks before helping the children or anyone else. You can't help anyone else without, first, helping yourself. If missing your family and friends results in you working to compensate for their love, is it really unconditional love?"

Ouch.

I learned to stop a lot of the behaviors that yielded self-sabotage and intentionally worked on creating an atmosphere of peace. Peace for me meant drawing healthy lines in the sand to create boundaries of self-preservation. Saying no to others was a greater yes for me. Getting there involved sitting and taking some time to see what I was really committed to and prioritizing those things. I began taking walks in the park with my music, being one with the Lord to clear my head in a healthy way. "Called to Be" by Jonathan Reynolds and "More of Thee, Less of Me" by Esther Smith were the two key songs I played on repeat during this transitional season as they re-affirmed my new identity.

I trained my ear to hear what God wanted to say to me in this season. This was a critical skill to stay in alignment with Him. Staying in alignment also meant being willing and obedient if He was to give me instructions. Well, he did. After working with a local community organization, they wanted to honor me with an award for donating pizzas, which was part of my role in field marketing.

I heard, *Take your mom with you, and have her bring her résumé.*

The move was a hard adjustment for my mom as well. She missed my other siblings, grandkids, and relationships she'd developed. And she'd become a full-time advocate against domestic violence in our home state and made many connections with advocacy organizations. She was a resident expert and powerhouse in domestic violence groups. Now, she was starting from ground zero.

"Mom, I'm getting an award on behalf of Domino's from an organization that works to fight against domestic violence, and they do a lot of teen initiatives. I want you to come with me and bring your résumé."

"I don't really feel like going," she said.

Mom was battling depression, which was common with a big move like this because she was isolated.

"I don't care; you're going. I feel a strong sense in my spirit that you're supposed to be in the room. Here's the information. See you there."

I left and headed to the event after I made a few impromptu

store visits to drop off marketing kits. Right before it was time to receive the award, I saw my mom walk into the room. As I accepted the award, I gave a shout out to her.

"I appreciate the work you're doing for the community, especially because I grew up in a home with domestic violence, and my mom is a survivor. She has joined me here today."

After the ceremony, my mom and the leader of the organization went off to a corner to have a conversation. I had to leave and get back to more store visits.

My mom called me. "Tiffany, she asked about my story and wanted to know about my advocacy experience. After I shared and told her I'm looking for a job in that area again, she asked me for my résumé and told me about a position that's open right in the field of domestic violence advocacy."

"That's great, Ma!"

"I'm on my way home to apply."

"Awesome! Keep me posted."

"Thank you for pushing me to come."

"Anytime, Ma."

I had no clue what was on the other side of that instruction. I just obeyed and was glad she obeyed.

My mom was the last person to apply to the job before the position closed, and she was hired within two weeks. God was blowing my mind even more. Mom was already walking in her purpose in Michigan, and now she was walking in her purpose in Arizona. I kept my ear attuned for more instructions.

I didn't approach my new role the traditional way because God was navigating me. Instead of coming into a market and implementing changes immediately with no buy-in, I assessed and had meetings. I took the time to learn my supervisors, managers, and employees. I wanted to know what drove them and why they chose these stores. My store visits were about driving change and coaching, but a lot of times, they were coaching me.

They were training my heart for compassion. A lot of the employees there had incredible stories about why they were where they were, stories of family, dedication, and health. As I showed them care and compassion, they, in exchange, demonstrated a drive and willingness to partner with me for the market. While there were necessary changes to be made, they were done and met with support.

I was partnered with a director who was also non-traditional. Upon meeting him, I noticed he wore a WWJD (What would Jesus do?) bracelet. I didn't work for him but was partnered with him to support his market. Our unconventional approaches were rooted in having a foundation in Christ, which led to us turning a negative sales market positive and becoming the number-one corporate market.

Outside of work, I finally found an amazing church, the church God intended for me. It was a hidden gem. I had searched all over Phoenix, and not once had it shown up on my radar. During a conversation with the former market coach, she recommended Faith Christian Center Phoenix. She mentioned she had visited a couple of times and a friend of hers was a member there.

I went to visit, and it was where I needed to be. The praise and worship, the sermon, and the people were amazing. Pastor Sean Moore preached on scheduling, and it felt like it was God talking to me directly.

"You have to have vision. What is the expectation of your calling? You're defined by this vision. You can't be a leader if you can't see vision. But you can't glorify the to-do list. Once you have the vision, break it down into bite-size pieces so your actions align with it. Then prioritize that vision. Make time for the most important things and say no to them rarely. Most Christians respond to the demands of all people, but Jesus chose His assignment carefully. His vision was placed over the demand and perceived need of people."

Stop right there! I said to myself. *This is confirmation for what my counselor has been working with me on. Stop prioritizing everything and everyone's vision over mine, for me to be more self-interested in this season. Okay, Tiff, refocus. Get back to paying attention. Carry on, Pastor Moore.*

"As a steward of your life, you have to prioritize this life God has designed for you. Scheduling is simply budgeting your time. Followers react to time, but leaders invest time, and their calendar is filled with priority. Your schedule shouldn't be built on tasks but by vision fulfillment. Without vision, all scheduling is monitoring your own busyness. Advancing to the next level requires a new schedule. Jesus had a schedule Himself, if you review His life timeline. If Jesus didn't say yes to everything, neither should we."

Wow! Talk about a sermon tailored for me. I didn't need to go to another church. This was my Phoenix church now. Every time the church doors opened, I was there. Not only did Pastor Moore preach a confirming word for me, but he gave scheduling tips that answered the question I had when Napoleon told me I needed to pivot to becoming more self-interested.

The move was now perfect. I had a church that would build upon the foundation I had started with Evangel. My excitement was uncontainable. I learned myself in Arizona, my likes and dislikes, how to do things for me and accomplish things I never saw myself accomplishing. I continued to pursue Christ in my singleness and maintain my purity along with counseling.

I phoned home and checked in with my goddad about how things were going, and he informed me that AJ was recently diagnosed with stage II non-Hodgkin lymphoma. My heart dropped. I scheduled a trip home because that was my homie. Though we didn't talk much, we talked enough. Upon landing back home, I mentally prepared myself as Pastor Bonner and I pulled up to the hospital and walked into his hospital room.

I came into the room to a laughing AJ because that's who he

is. We greeted each other instantly with a hug. I was taken aback because I thought people were supposed to be sad and down when they were sick, especially with cancer. Not AJ. He had his bible study books in the bed with him and shared with us how he was even ministering to the nurses and those he encountered.

"Either God is going to heal me on this side of heaven, or I'm going to go home with Him and sleep. Either way, healing is mine."

I had never witnessed such great faith. I'd read about it a couple of times in the Bible, but I had never seen it with my own eyes.

"I miss the praise and worship and sermons, though. Y'all know my spirit needs to be fed," he said.

"Say no more; I got you," I said.

My goddad looked at me with surprise, and when we left, I shared with him my plan. "I'm going to reach out to Gina and see if she can get him CDs of the worship and the Word. And now is the time to get live streaming activated for the church. He can be our tester."

Pastor Bonner looked as if he couldn't believe I had developed a plan so quickly, but he smiled and agreed.

While testing the church's streaming service, AJ and I talked a lot more. I hated that I was so far from him while he was going through chemo treatments, so I taught him how to Skype during our testing and feedback sessions. The first time we Skyped, I saw a hairless AJ, and I had to fight back tears.

"I look like a baby dragon," he said, laughing.

"No, you don't. You still look like cute AJ."

I hated seeing him like that, but I was glad to see his spirits were still up. Chemo left him very weak, so we didn't Skype as often as we used to. One day, he mentioned that he was shoveling snow. I was against it and called Pastor Bonner on him.

"AJ needs help. Can you send someone to do his snow while he's undergoing chemo sessions? Also, you know how he loves the worship department. Can you schedule a worship department visit?"

"Sure. That's not a bad idea. We will sing some Christmas carols."

AJ absolutely loved the surprise. Months later, he was declared cancer free, and I flew home for the celebration service. He did a special video interview and shared his testimony. At the end of the video, he sang William McDowell's "I Belong to You," one of the choir songs for which he sang lead solo before his cancer diagnosis.

I was in tears and gave him the biggest hug when he finished and came off the stage. Pastor Bonner needed an assistant and selected AJ. He wanted me to train him. AJ was open and ready for it. Our conversations were much more frequent as I trained him on the processes of the department and the ways of my goddad. After department business, we talked about our sermon takeaways, a worship song we were listening to, and our spiritual growth learnings.

That was always our common ground. He began sharing more about his family, his divorce process, the women who were interested in him, his feelings about the dating process, and desiring to be in the center of God's will. I, too, shared takeaways from my past relationships, the learnings I gained from my move to Phoenix, and how I was exactly where he was, wanting to be in the center of God's will for my life. AJ encouraged me to take some time out for me, to not be all about working hard and no play. Outside of work travel, I never traveled anywhere for myself.

I decided to take a trip for my thirtieth birthday to Kailua-Kona Hawaii by myself in 2014. This was the longest flight I'd been on and with no Wi-Fi. Though scared, I was set to enjoy myself. I took a ton of pictures, rested, relaxed, ate a lot, and went sightseeing. I did a lot of reading while at the hotel pool and listened to the ocean waves. I observed a lot of couples while on vacation, and my spirit wanted to become sad because I longed for that. But I snapped myself out of it by writing out a list of characteristics I wanted in a husband and prayed over it. I was in paradise. I wasn't about to let loneliness ruin this trip for me.

Some of my favorite moments were randomly pulling over while driving to capture pictures of the beautiful ocean views, relaxing on a black sand beach, visiting the botanical garden and waterfall, and going on the ocean bottom tour where I saw many beautiful fish and even a sleeping shark. The luau and hidden hole-in-the-wall food places satisfied my taste pallets. Almost everyone I encountered was amazed I was there alone. I was content, as this was my first time truly disconnecting from everyone.

Upon my return, I oversaw the planning of my goddad's surprise sixtieth birthday party, which required me to come back into town again. AJ and I worked closely to orchestrate the worship and media department's celebration. AJ pulled off an amazing party at the church for Pastor Bonner. At the end, he gave me the tightest hug while looking into my eyes.

"Thank you so much for your help," he said.

My feelings were turning for AJ, but I told myself, *No, Tiffany, you will not do this.* Then my godsister walked up, and said, "AJ likes you!"

"What? No. He's the homie. No!"

"No, he likes you. It's in his eyes. Y'all have a chemistry."

"No, we don't. When I thought of liking him that way, Dad said no, so it's no."

"I'm going to talk to Dad."

"No!"

She didn't listen, and she asked him, but my goddad's response was still no. I continued to keep AJ in the friend zone and decided to put some distance between us to protect my heart. Two months passed, and I had to fly back into town for a corporate meeting at the top of January 2015. After my meetings, I normally extended my travel to stay the weekends so I could visit. While driving to the church to sit in on choir rehearsal, I received a call that my best friend's mom, who was the wife of Pastor Bonner's son, was terminally ill.

Tears streamed down my face. I texted AJ and asked him to come into the office. He came in, and as I tried to talk, he leaned over and kissed me on my forehead, hugging me while rocking our bodies like a synchronized dance. He wouldn't let go until I laughed.

He went back downstairs to the choir rehearsal room.

I was lost inside the world of AJ. I had forgotten to tell him to get my goddad to come up or even tell him why I was crying. I called him again, and he came up for me to deliver the message.

I prayed on my drive back to the house where I was staying while in town. "You know I've been walking down singleness and purity, but I have feelings toward AJ, and I'm laying it out to You. He's going to have to pursue me differently than any other man I've dated. If he isn't who You have for me, then I don't want him. I'm content with just getting a dog and being single if he isn't Your will. Show me if this is to be explored."

21

Ready for Love

A DAY LATER, IT was Sunday, church day. It was awkward to be around AJ knowing my feelings for him were rising. AJ came into the office being himself, greeting me with a hug and putting on his headphones to listen to his music. He was to lead a song that day. I took a picture without him knowing, and my flash almost gave me away. I had to leave during second service to get to the airport.

Before I left, one of the ladies had us take a picture, and the picture of us was telling of our bond. On the ride to the airport, I stared and smiled at the picture. We looked like we were a couple. While sitting at my gate, I received a text from AJ stating that my visits back home were never long enough, and he was considering visiting Arizona. My insides were giddy, but I kept it cool; he was just being nice.

I arrived back home during the week of the Super Bowl, which was being hosted by Arizona. I shared with AJ all the activities, from sending pictures to getting him a commemorative t-shirt. I had to leave town midweek to help my best friend with the funeral service for her mom. AJ didn't miss a beat with texting me. The tide of communication had changed. We texted each other all day and evening that entire week, talking about every subject imaginable. During prior communications, he'd told me how much he disliked talking on the phone and texting.

I shared with him the happenings of the upcoming Super Bowl, and he shared with me more about his workday and the evening dinners he was preparing. I was still working while away because Super Bowl week meant a lot of sales for our stores. I had also received tickets to the Super Bowl, but I couldn't go because I was going out of town. My director and I brainstormed a week-long competition to get the stores pumped and award one of the store managers the tickets to the game.

AJ couldn't believe it. "You mean to tell me you have Super Bowl tickets, and you're not going?" he said.

"Well, it's more important for me to be here with my bestie, but I wouldn't have wanted to go with anyone but you, anyway," I said.

"You wanna go with me or you wanna *go* with me?"

I froze. I had a choice—front or tell the truth.

"Hey, wait, Tiff," he said, "you're actually thinking about it?"

"I'm going to call you back in a little bit."

I knew the trajectory of our relationship was about to change. I was wrong; AJ continued to text me regularly like nothing happened. I finally sent him a long text message explaining how I felt and left the decision up to him.

Lord, you know where my heart is. If it ain't of You, I don't want it.

AJ responded with a series of wows. "But you're my friend; how would that work?"

"I don't know, but this is where I'm at with it," I replied.

He took some time before responding. I was already preparing myself for rejection. *Welp, this wasn't of God.*

After some hours, he called. "All right, let's go," he said.

"Huh?"

"Let's go; let's do this. Say it with me now: I'm your man."

I was speechless. I didn't see that coming. He shared with

me how he'd processed his decision. He was mostly concerned about losing his friend if it didn't work until another friend said to him, "But AJ, what if it's God?"

Unbeknownst to me, he'd made a list, too, and everything he wanted in a wife and bonus mom for his daughters, I encompassed; plus, we already had three years of friendship under our belt.

It was important for me to put my cards out there first. "I'm not having sex until marriage. No pictures, nothing," I said.

"Okay, cool. Sex isn't an issue for me." And with that, he went on to talking about the next subject.

During my single period, when talking to guys, I intentionally led off with my purity vow, and they'd instantly say they didn't want to continue talking. That was cool with me because it weeded out those I wasn't meant to be with.

AJ and I started talking day and night about everything under the moon. He even frequently sang random songs to me that melted my heart.

We had similar family circumstances, and although we were fourteen years apart in age, we had so much in common. One of the things I liked the most was that he couldn't wait until I got out of church because he wanted to hear my sermon notes. I never had someone so invested in my spiritual walk to share that part of me with. We talked about past hurts, past relationship issues, and the importance of shaping our future based on Christ. That led to us discussing the ground rules for our relationship. Out the gate, AJ was headstrong: "It's you, me, and God. Team three."

While on the phone one night, he proposed by serenading me with a medley: "You're So Beautiful" by Jussie Smollet mixed with "Forever My Lady" by Jodeci.

I said yes!

We discussed wedding dates and considered August, then I declared that I didn't want to have a wedding.

"Are you sure? This is your first wedding, honey," AJ said.

"Yeah, but I hate party planning. I'm still paying off student loans, and I don't want to pay all that money. We can do something later for our anniversary, but I'd rather just get it done. I'll be in town in three weeks for work. Want to get married then? What's the difference in getting married in March vs. August? And we don't want to tempt ourselves or appear to be doing wrong during my visits back."

"Sure, let's do it!" AJ sounded so excited.

"Huh, you sure? You answered so fast. You don't want to pray on it some more? I know you've been married before, and I don't want to rush you."

"I'm a grown man. I know what I want, and I don't have to wait because I'm sure in my decision. I prayed already, which is how we ended up here. You date to marry. This was my end goal, choosing you, and I'm with it."

Well, okay. I was so used to guys being fickle in their decision making and inconsistent. Here I was now in the face of certainty and consistency. I didn't want to share my decision with anyone because I didn't want outside opinions. I only talked to my mom about it beforehand.

"Tiffany, you're grown. If you want to go to the courthouse and get married, then go," she said.

On March 12, 2015, I flew back into town on a redeye and landed at six a.m. I was so excited and anxious as I drove to his house. *This is the day it's going to happen,* I thought. *I'm about to be a married woman! So, this is what happens when I stop trying to orchestrate my future. This fine, funny, tenor swept me off my feet.*

We made the drive to the courthouse and said, "I Do."

It felt surreal, but I was thrilled. We didn't kiss or have sex until after we sealed the deal. I said what I was going to do, and I did it, all for the glory of God.

We didn't make our marriage public knowledge based on bad advice someone had given us surrounding the fact that

I was still living in Phoenix. But we told our core circle of family and friends, especially since I had changed my name immediately upon returning to Phoenix.

22

It Worked Out for My Good

I IMMEDIATELY TOLD MY job that I was married, and they were excited for me. Management promised to work on getting me back into the same state with my new husband. We alternated visits between Detroit and Phoenix every two weeks until I was promoted and relocated back to Michigan to my new home with AJ.

Within two weeks of being married, my manager called me to tell me I'd been awarded the Marketing Coach of the Year Award for 2014, and the award ceremony would be in Las Vegas. When I thought God couldn't blow my mind anymore, He kept on. Receiving that award was just a visual representation of what God had done in that market through me. AJ was genuinely happy and supportive of me as my husband.

It felt great to be with a man who wasn't threatened by my successes, supported me, and even challenged me to be better. Shortly after I received the call, they promoted me again to advertising specialist. I was humbled beyond imagination. I had started at the company as a contractor with no experience, but the skills and giftings I possessed made room for me in each role and department. I was now on a team working behind the scenes with creative agencies to manage our television commercials, timelines, and everything customer facing in the stores.

No one can tell me God isn't real. I've seen His hand move on my life way too many times to imagine, from my healing, to my spiritual evolution, to receiving the greatest blessing after salvation through my marriage to AJ and the two beautiful adult bonus daughters I inherited.

AJ made it comfortable for me to love and provided a safe space for me. He allowed me to be nothing but myself. During our early days of marriage, I struggled with trying to measure up to the model of a wife my mother displayed for me and was driving myself to exhaustion. But AJ had no expectations for me, only to be who I was, and we would navigate what our marriage looked like together.

Though AJ received a healthy and whole wife, ongoing counseling work was needed for this new season.

I had new triggers connected to things I didn't know I needed healing from that were exposed in the early months of our marriage. I quickly learned that the work is never done, but when you're armed with the tools to do the work, it makes the process better. AJ's patience and grace as I worked through it was insurmountable. We became accountable to Pastor Brooks and his wife, Yodit, and participated in marriage counseling to strengthen our foundation. Being spiritually grounded with AJ allowed me more freedom to be a whole person. I'm now able to love and forgive from a level I didn't think was imaginable. The work is still ongoing, but we've made significant progress through the years.

Becoming an instant bonus mom to two daughters in their early and mid-twenties was intimidating at first, and anxiety flooded my heart because I wasn't sure how they'd feel, yet AJ wasn't worried.

"God put us together, and you don't have to worry about that," he said.

I took my time getting to know them, not forcing anything. It was never my goal to replace my bonus daughters' moms; I sought to have my own relationship with them. I love to create memorable experiences for those closest to me, so during our first year, I wanted to create family memories. Regardless of my parents' divorce, I was raised on the model of familyhood, and even when my siblings and I didn't get along, there was no way we could go long periods of time without speaking, and we always had each other's back. I suggested family dinners, birthday celebrations, and holidays to get to know each other.

My favorite moments with my family were the get togethers. The first gathering I planned was for Father's Day to celebrate AJ. Our oldest daughter lives out of state with our two grandsons, but was able to come into town, and both bonus daughters were present. It was a collection of beautiful moments filled with laughter, games, and good eats.

The next big event was AJ's birthday. I needed help with my vision, and our youngest daughter was down to help. We went to Party City and had a ball, and after party planning, we went to eat. During our dinner conversation, I realized how deeply impacted she was by her parents' divorce. Listening to her reminded me of myself and the feelings I had about my parents. She tried to detour the conversation because it can be awkward. I understood that, but I asked her to continue. AJ had told me a lot anyway, but I wanted her perspective.

I was that kid who watched my parents' divorce and saw the ripple effect, so it was an important moment between us. I cried with her and shared with her my background to show that I understood her feelings. At that moment, I realized this wouldn't be the last time I shared my story. My pain had purpose.

In my spirit, I received yet another prompt to pick up the

manuscript I began writing in 2006. When I was in college, I wrote it from the perspective of an angry, hurting young girl, but now, I wanted to rewrite it from a place of wholeness. The conversation with my bonus daughter was the kick off for me to start sharing my story often with other women, men, teenagers, and even strangers who related to my message. Where my misery lay, my ministry was being birthed.

A Letter to Tiffany

Dear Tiffany,

I am giving you everything I believe will help you through all the seasons you've gone through:

Scared Little Tiff, it doesn't make sense now, but I promise you it will. Your mom is going to be okay. She will live and not die; she's going to come out much stronger. Even though it's hard, keep your smile, and don't let the circumstances and the things you're witnessing change who you are at the core. For those who are supposed to be a safe haven for you both, don't let their words, stares, and judgmental statements define who you are. Crying is okay; don't bottle it up. God sees you. It's easy to hate your mom right now, but don't. She's trying to survive. When you're afraid, continue to keep your teddy bear close and imagine that's how God is hugging you during those hard moments. Keep coloring to clear your mind, and don't stop having big dreams.

Angry Tiff, it hurts, I get it. No one understands you or sees you, and everyone judges you. You aren't any of those things they say. These experiences are giving you insight so you can later provide a greater compassion to children who will be where you are later on. You're going to be a voice for those kids who feel *Forgotten*. In the meantime, continue listening to music, but make sure the lyrics are giving you hope, not dragging you down into a sultry pit.

Young Adult Tiff, self-aware and confused, "When your dad and mother forsake you, the Lord will take of you" (Psalms 27:10). God is going to get you to a place of restoration. He's seeing what you're going through, from the abuse, to the divorce, to your dad's remarriage. Psychologists tell us the way we choose to interpret what happens in our lives, more than the actual circumstances, determines our destiny. Bitter or better—You get to decide. Be better. Speak life into what your life will be. "God knows the plans He has for us, and it's one that's filled with hope and a promise!" (Jeremiah 29:11, ERV). "Before you were even shaped in the womb, He knew all about you" (Jeremiah 1:5, MSG). Don't allow what broke you or what you watched break others be associated to your destiny. God isn't a God of condemnation. He understands we miss the mark daily, and there is no perfect Christian. A relationship with Christ is not about perfection; it's about consistently pursuing the things that please Him and allowing Him to put his super on our natural. Put your focus on Him and receive His love for you, so you can love others like He loves you. The grace He extends to you, He will need you to extend to others and, most importantly, your family. Listen to Travis Greene's song, "Intentional." What comes to mind as you listen to those lyrics? I see you hiding behind your title and ambitions, but don't let those things define you. Once you come out of your ego and pride and allow the Holy Spirt to flow through your life, you will be a light in Corporate America.

Congratulations on your Christ-centered healing in love, Tiff. You will be a blessing and make an impact for the Kingdom from the things you learn. You won't believe this, but you're going to be a resource for others and a trusted advisor to help others launch and define their businesses. All of your learnings in these environments will help you create a lane for yourself, and you're going to thrive. Everything that has transpired in your life, good and bad, has been intentional for the Kingdom of Heaven. Your talents and abilities are being orchestrated for your purpose. The main gift you've had since a little girl will be used to touch nations. The essay you began in the last semester of college will be developed into a book. Your book is a tool in God's arsenal to deliver help and hope. You matter, and your circumstances aren't the final say on your life. There's a depth of revelation you can't tap into by hiding behind corporate accolades. It requires a greater vulnerability.

Continue to stay consistent with counseling. Do the work and heal. There will be an intense amount of pressure, but be confident. God is working with you to steady your heart and mind. Transitions are usually difficult, and this is designed to build your character in a unique way. God will teach you to lean on Him more than you ever have. Trust the unexpected over what you could expect. Be proud of yourself for not listening to those who told you not to go. You chose to save yourself and be self-interested. This is an important moment. God is pushing you to develop a deeper level of trust. Operating in your own strength won't work in this season. He will order your steps and blow your mind. Treasure the new quiet moments. Don't try to fill your days with noise and busyness. In these quiet moments, when you've settled yourself, your emotions will become unearthed. These moments of settling refine your posture of worship to access Him. These are moments where you will be settled in the eye of the storm. You must stay connected to the gift of Him. When you're in tune with worship, you're able to establish so much more with great results.

Though you've had your heart broken on many levels, those invaluable lessons have prepared you for this day with your new husband. You will find vulnerability in your confidence birthed from your security in God and self. You will be able to trust your heart with this man and learn what vulnerability looks like with him. You didn't think you could do it, but because you used your singleness for Christ's glory, you were rewarded with a husband "after Christ's own heart who will love you as Christ loves the church" (Ephesians 5:25, TPT). You see how everything you've been through connects? You're able to see order in the midst of chaos, orchestrate harmony from disharmony, extend compassion and care in a careless environment, and give direction to those unable to see what the next steps should be. You got this, and just like Sarah Jakes-Roberts says, "Bruised heels still crush serpents' heads!"

Love Always,
Tiffany

To the Forgotten

THE HEALING AND HAPPINESS that comes in moving forward and not looking back brings so much peace and purpose. It may not look or feel like it, but all pain has a purpose. God loves you, and you aren't *Forgotten*! You may have gone through or maybe you're still going through some hard life challenges. Even through your missteps, He loves you, and He has a plan for your life and a plan for the hurt not to overtake you.

Once you grab ahold of the purpose, pushing past the pain is the goal, so you can enjoy the life you're called to live. Connection with the heart and mouth is all that's needed to accept salvation and have your name written in heaven. Say it, believe it, and you will have it. Say what you want, not what you don't want.

My life is a story of grace amid the struggles. At the tender age of eighteen, I found myself broken by life. My family unit, which I relied on for my life, left me uncovered, naked, and feeling helpless, leading me to run into the arms of the wrong men and unhealthy situations to compensate. The issues I encountered were connected to my identity. I thought my identity was wrapped in my family and who I thought we were as a family unit. So if my family unit was no more, who was I?

I tried answering my question of identity through culture, the songs I filled my spirit with, job titles, a fleeting image of what society said I should be versus who God already said I was. I was fearfully and wonderfully made. As I found out more intimately about how the Lord redeems the time and restores the years we feel were wasted, the motivation to hold onto those things as crutches left me. I wanted to pursue Godliness, healing, and purpose.

As Greg Harden told me, "There's too much to your story to not be successful." I got to become a redefined version of myself based on the Word. I know God isn't done evolving me, and I know He's waiting to do the same for you. If you haven't made that change just yet, all you need to do is decide. It had to stop somewhere generationally, and I chose for it to stop with me.

Acknowledgement is key. From there, you can attribute certain behaviors and attitudes to key life events that may have caused you to do things that don't reflect the best of you. Per the National Coalition Against Domestic Violence, "Children who witness incidents of domestic violence (a form of childhood trauma) are at greater risk of serious health problems, including obesity, cancer, heart disease, depression, substance abuse, tobacco use, and unintended pregnancies, than peers who did not witness domestic violence."

I quickly identified myself in that statement, and if I hadn't taken a stand and said enough was enough, it would've been my end story. But thanks be unto God, He knew His purpose and calling was greater, and He knew I would now be using the pains of my past to help someone else who is already going through it or prevent them from travelling that road through my awareness. I refuse to let the generational curse continue. It is my goal to make it stop with me.

There are pivotal points in your life when you must decide to press past the memories and pain to accomplish the course your life is meant to take. You must retrain your brain after witnessing the trauma and choose not to continue keeping yourself in the victim seat as an excuse not to heal. I was given a new heart. I once felt it would be a clear defining act, a miracle from God if my heart changed. Well, throughout the years, God did soften my hardened heart layer by layer.

I was able to forgive my dad and his wife and make conscious efforts toward reconciliation. Walking in healing and forgiveness gave me a choice. I didn't have to keep seeing my dad through the lens of painful memories of the past but through the lens of Christ's grace and the ability to let go. It's a consistent effort of intentionality, but I keep God's Word at my heart, even if some people cannot accept my truth.

I transitioned from a routine church goer to a relationship with Christ when I got the revelation that my salvation was not based on my dad, but my Heavenly Dad. Grabbing ahold of that revelation changed everything. I began to love and give grace like God shows me.

Out of all I've endured, I came to have a real relationship with Christ that continues to grow. Even with the flaws of family, church members, friends, etc., those things don't dictate my love, adoration, and life of worship for Him. That was when my freedom was released, and my deliverance broke through to have a peace that transcends all human comprehension.

Your feelings are valid, but don't allow them to stay there. Don't allow those feelings to keep you in a place of unhealthiness. Don't allow those circumstances to change you into someone you weren't meant to be. Don't allow them to prohibit you from the life God has called you to live and relationships He's called you to have. Do the work to overcome by going to counseling, build a trusted village that will help you heal and move forward.

Accepting my imperfections and God's reckless love for me was life changing. I remember in my younger years reflecting on my past and regretting my past actions. Why did I feel the need to prove myself? Why did I need validation so badly? Why did I need to be so hard?

Being older, I accepted and embraced those early years. I'm not proud of the missteps I took, but even in all these "wrong" things, purpose was birthed. Because I was so hard, I'm able to identify with those who are hard. I'm also able to show a deeper compassion for those who are written off. I'm able to speak life into those who feel the need to prove themselves.

If you choose to believe and make the best life investment there is, please pray the following prayer:

Dear Lord,

Thank you for loving me so much that You sent your Son to die for me and for confirming Your Word that whomever believes in Him will not perish but have eternal life. Please forgive me of my sins. Your Word says we're saved by grace through faith as a gift from You. I believe and confess with my mouth that Jesus Christ is Your Son and the Savior of the world. I believe He died on the cross for me, rose on the third day, and is alive and coming back. I am saved and will spend eternity with You. In Jesus's name, I pray. Amen.

Resources

National Domestic Violence (24/7)
If you or someone you know is experiencing domestic violence, please contact the National Domestic Violence hotline.
Website: https://www.thehotline.org/
Phone: 800-799-7233
Please note: The Hotline does not give legal advice nor are they legal advocates. They may be able to help you locate a legal advocate in your area if needed.

Legal Help
If you determine that taking legal action against an abusive partner is the best course for you, visit the following website for next steps:
Website: https://www.thehotline.org/help/legal-help/

Safety Plan
A safety plan is a personalized, practical plan that includes ways to remain safe while in a relationship, planning to leave, or after you leave. Safety planning involves how to cope with emotions, tell friends and family about the abuse, take legal action, and more.
https://www.thehotline.org/help/path-to-safety/

Recommended Scriptures

SEEDS ARE PLANTED AND power is released when you say scripture and memorize it in your mind, heart, and soul. I even encourage you to make it personal. Where you see "you," replace with your name or "I." The Lord is faithful to His Word.

Fear/Worry

- Joshua 1:9 – "Be strong and courageous. Do not be afraid; don't be discouraged, for the Lord your God will be with you wherever you go."
- 2 Timothy 1:7 – "For the Spirit of God has not given us a spirit of fear, but of power, love and self-discipline."
- Psalm 23:4 – "Even though you walk through the darkest valley, you will fear no evil for you are with me; your rod and staff, they comfort me."
- 1 Peter 3:14 – "But even if you should suffer for what is right, you are blessed. 'Do not fear their threats; do not be frightened.'"
- Isaiah 35:4 – "Say to those with fearful hearts, 'Be strong, do not fear; your God will come, he will come with vengeance; with divine retribution he will come to save you.'"

Anger

- Ephesians 4:26 – "In your anger do not sin …"
- James 1:19-20 – "Everyone should be quick to listen, slow to speak and slow to become angry, because human anger does not produce the righteousness that God desires."
- Proverbs 29:11 – "Fools give full vent to their rage, but the wise bring calm in the end."

Newness

- 2 Corinthians 5:17 – "Therefore, if anyone is in Christ, the new creation has come: The old has gone, the new is here!"
- Lamentations 3:22-24 – :Because of the Lord's great love, we are not consumed, for his compassions never fail. They are new every morning; great is your faithfulness. I say to myself, 'The Lord is my portion; therefore, I will wait for him.'"
- Job 8:7 – "Your beginnings will seem humble, so prosperous will your future be."

Love

- 1 John 4:7-8 – "Dear friends, let us love one another, for love comes from God. Everyone who loves has been born of God and knows God. Whoever does not love does not know God, because God is love."
- Jeremiah 31:3 – "The Lord appeared to us in the past, saying: 'I have loved you with an everlasting love; I have drawn you with unfailing kindness.'"

- John 3:16 – "For God so loved the world that he gave his one and only Son, that whoever believes in him shall not perish but have eternal life."

Forgiveness

- Matthew 6:14-15 – "For if you forgive other people when they sin against you, your heavenly dad will also forgive you. But if you do not forgive others their sins, your dad will not forgive your sins."
- Luke 17:3-4 – "So watch yourselves. If your brother or sister sins against you, rebuke them; if they repent, forgive them. Even if they sin against you seven times in a day and seven times come back to you saying, 'I repent,' you must forgive them."
- Ephesians 4:31-32 – "Get rid of all bitterness, rage and anger, brawling and slander, along with every form of malice. Be kind and compassionate to one another, forgiving each other, just as in Christ God forgave you."

Confidence

- Isaiah 40:31 – "But those who hope in the Lord will renew their strength. They will soar on wings like eagles; they will run and not grow weary; they will walk and not be faint."
- Mark 11:24 – "Therefore I tell you, whatever you ask for in prayer, believe that you have received it, and it will be yours."
- Psalm 23:1-6 – "The LORD is my shepherd, I lack nothing. He makes me lie down in green pastures, he leads me beside quiet waters, he refreshes my soul. He guides me along the right paths for his name's sake. Even though I walk through the darkest valley, I will fear

no evil, for you are with me; your rod and your staff, they comfort me. You prepare a table before me in the presence of my enemies. You anoint my head with oil; my cup overflows. Surely, your goodness and love will follow me all the days of my life, and I will dwell in the house of the LORD forever."

Restoration

- Isaiah 61:7 – "Instead of your shame, you will receive a double portion, and instead of disgrace, you will rejoice in your inheritance. And so you will inherit a double portion in your land, and everlasting joy will be yours."
- Jeremiah 30:17 – "But I will restore health and heal your wounds declares the Lord…"
- Joel 2:25-26 – "I will repay you for the years the locusts have eaten— the great locust and the young locust, the other locusts and the locust swarm — my great army that I sent among you. You will have plenty to eat, until you are full, and you will praise the name of the LORD your God, who has worked wonders for you; never again will my people be shamed."

About the Author

TIFFANY MENSAH IS A woman of faith, author, advocate, marketing maven, and entrepreneur. With ten-plus years in Corporate America, she currently works as a marketing project manager while owning and operating Mensah & Co., a creative consulting agency. Tiffany is most proud of the work she's done personally and spiritually to address the childhood trauma and PTSD she experienced while growing up in a home plagued by domestic violence. This work has fueled her to launch DOVES Network (Daily Overcoming Violence & Embracing Safety), a 501(c)(3) dedicated to the prevention of domestic violence and childhood domestic violence exposure through awareness and outreach programs.

Tiffany loves spending time with her family and her fur baby, Shadow, and snapping candid photos to capture the moment. You may also find her relaxing to a good playlist while she zones out and creates. Tiffany is dedicated to enjoying the life she has built with her husband and continuing to evolve in her personal development.

CONNECT WITH TIFFANY MENSAH

Website: www.TiffanyMensah.com
Facebook: www.facebook.com/tiffanymauthor
Instagram: @tiffanymauthor
Youtube: Tiffany Mensah
iTunes Playlist: *You are not Forgotten*

Made in United States
Orlando, FL
01 January 2022

12714006R00155